Curious Sussex

Overleaf: *Lewes Castle*

Curious Sussex

MARY DELORME

Photographs by Jon Delorme

© *Mary Delorme 1987*
First published in Great Britain 1987

Robert Hale Limited
Clerkenwell House
Clerkenwell Green
London ECIR OHT

British Library Cataloguing in Publication Data
Delorme, Mary
   Curious Sussex.
   1. Curiosities and wonders – England –
Sussex 2. Sussex – Miscellanea
I. Title
001.9′3′094225   AG243

ISBN 0-7090-2970-5

Set in Sabon by Rowland Phototypesetting Limited
Printed in Great Britain by
St Edmundsbury Press Limited, Bury St Edmunds, Suffolk
and bound by WBC Bookbinders Limited

Contents

List of Illustrations	7
Acknowledgements	9
1 Landmarks	13
2 Postdogs, Ponds, and Other Utilities	40
3 Man's Inhumanity to Man . . .	64
4 . . . and Otherwise	71
5 Paradoxically	91
6 Architecturally	108
7 Mainly Horticultural	140
8 Name-dropping	160
9 Glory, Alleluia	175
Bibliography	204
Index	205

In loving memory of
the veteran
John Delorme

Illustrations

Lewes Castle	*frontispiece*
The Raptackle, Bosham	15
Bramber Castle	16
Bodiam Castle	20
Herstmonceux	22
Martello Tower	25
Racton Tower	27
Chanctonbury Ring	30
V for Victoria, Streat	33
The Long Man of Wilmington	34
White horse on High and Over Hill	36
The Seven Sisters	39
Springwells and Dog Lane	42
Chithurst Hammer Pond	43
Chanctonbury Dew Pond	46
Hastings' net shops	50
The University of Sussex	51
Mad Jack's pyramid	53
Plaques and tombstones	55
Woolavington church	58
The Russian Memorial	60
The Chattri Memorial	62
Harting's stocks and whipping post	65
Saddlescombe blind house	67
Tide Mills	69
Mad Jack's Wall	72
Chichester Market Cross	76
The Writer's church	79
Glyndebourne	85
Elsted church	92
The Cathedral of the Downs	94
The grave of Canute's daughter	97
New town planning at Winchelsea	99
Bluebell Halt	101

Amberley Wild Brooks	103
The Cokelers' chapel at Loxwood	106
Clergy House	109
The Alfriston Star	111
Smugglers' Cottage, Northiam	114
Brickwall House, Northiam	116
Ashcombe Toll House	117
Alciston Tithe Barn	121
Chailey Moat	124
Dickensian flavour at Castle Goring	126
Graeco-Palladian façade at Castle Goring	127
Half a church at Lullington	130
Medieval glass at Westham	135
Bramber lychgate	136
St Mary's, Bramber	137
Pyecombe church and crook	138
Woods Mill	146
The Ancestors	149
Chalkpit Garden, Highdown	154
The Church in a Wood	165
Jack and Jill went up the hill . . .	168
Maison Dieu, Arundel	177
The Chichester Moon	178
Silent kissing gate at Clapham church	180
Kissing gate in Clapham Woods	181
Barnlands, Lindfield village	185
Anne of Cleves' house at Ditchling	186
Anne of Cleves' house at Lewes	186
The Royal Pavilion, Brighton, under repair	190
The Amaranthine Palace	194
Tortington Priory	198
Moated Michelham	199
Tangmere	201

Maps

Sussex	10–11
1610 Speede map of Sussex	158–9

Acknowledgements

With pleasure, I acknowledge my debt to the many people who took an active interest in this book.

The assistance of Carolynne Dean and Harold Rogers was of particular value; Jim Cleland's theory on Mad Jack's illegal activities is entrancing, and he may yet convince me. The graciousness of Mrs Hatcher will long remain in my memory; few people, these days, so kindly make friends with a stranger.

Woods Mill caught my imagination and that of my photographer son; Mike Russell, the Warden, frequently let us in and chatted with a splendid disregard for official hours.

Many clergy have answered unexpected phone calls, and the staffs of the County Record Offices assisted with their usual expertise. Sister Julian of Hengrave Hall and Hazel Gage of Firle Place were generous with time and trouble, while John Creasey of Reading University gave valuable help on agricultural problems. The letter from the owner of the Perigoe Museum can only be described as a pearl beyond price.

The making of the book has given me many new friends, and cemented old friendships. I apologize in advance for any errors therein; even so, I hope that readers will experience some of the pleasure I found in writing it.

Permission has kindly been granted by Messrs Faber to quote from F. C. Stern, *The Chalk Garden*, and by Porter Prints of Harrogate to reproduce Speede/Sussex map 1610.

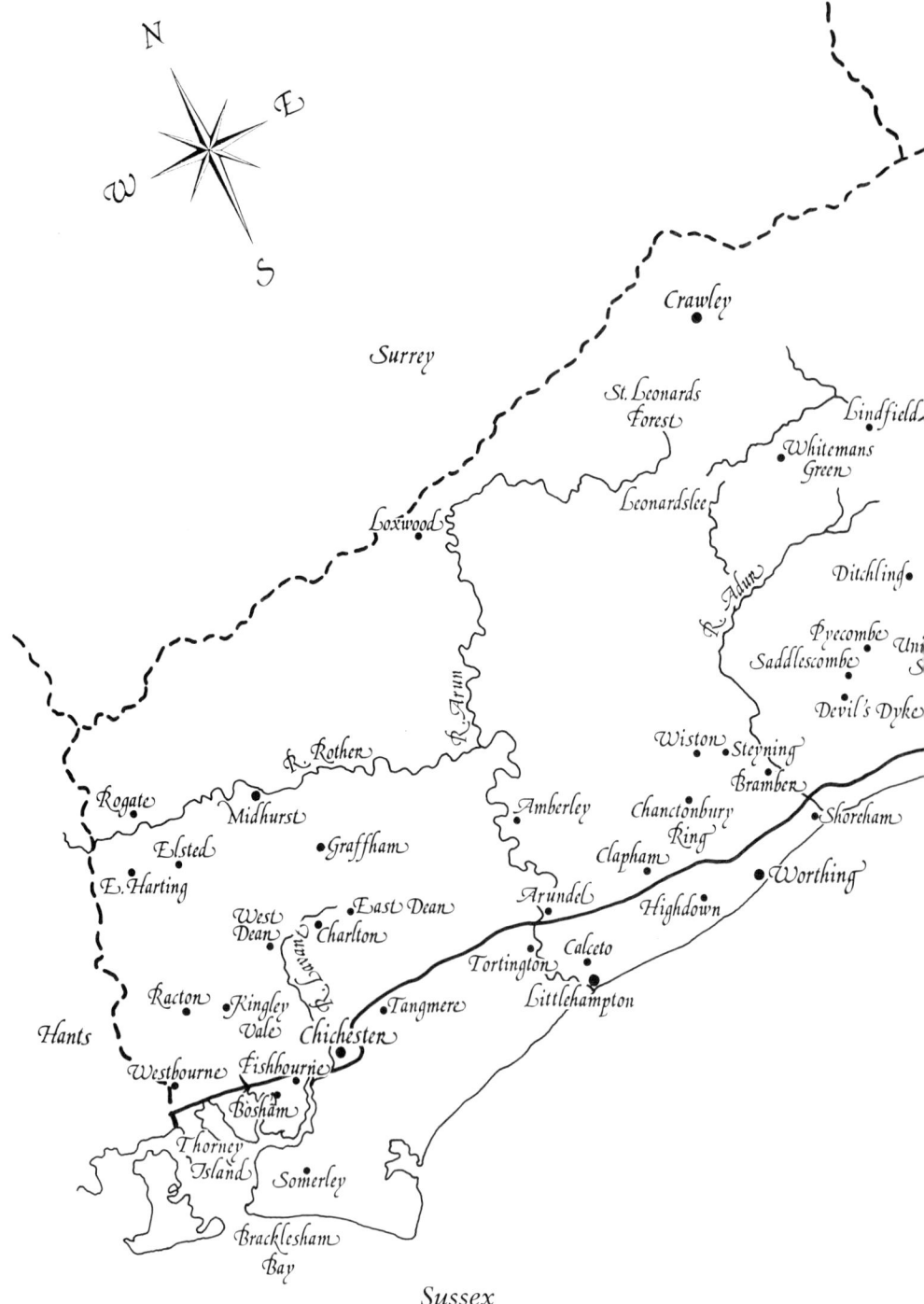

Kent

Eridge • Bodiam • Northiam R. Tillingham Rye
 • Ewhurst Rye Bay
R. Rother Sedlescombe •Winchelsea
 (Pestalozzi) R. Brede
Dallington Mountfield
Forest Cackle
 Street Battle
•Cackle Street Netherfield
Cross in Hand Three Cups
Heathfield Corner
ebell Rly Hastings
 •Ninfield
•Isfield Herstmonceux
 •Bexhill
R. Cuckmere
R. Ouse •Glyndebourne •Pevensey
•Lewes
Offham W. Firle Wilmington Lullington
reat High Church •Eastbourne
 & Oven Charleston Manor
 Westdean East
Brighton •Peacehaven Tide Mills Dean Beachy
 Newhaven Head

0 — 4 — 8 — 12 mls

1 Landmarks

Sussex has always been the fast lane for intending invaders, and each succeeding group to arrive in England needed to create its own defences. The sea was a major bastion, but the ancient hill forts provided high vantage points for look-out and defence. The charioteers of the British prince Cassivellaunus gained such devastating expertise through his rigorous lessons in advanced driving that they almost defeated Julius Caesar, but the Romans' luck held. Sussex still has a great deal of Roman building, including fortifications.

When William of Normandy planned his 1066 invasion, he knew of a useful Roman fort at Pevensey. A thousand years had left some deterioration, but it was close to that ideal landing-beach. William brought over parts of a castle in kit form; hefty panels, prefabricated in wood, to reinforce the crumbling Roman walls. His men were able to rest, eat and be organized before marching the short distance to Senlac, where they fought the October battle against Harold. It was an even closer contest than the struggle between Cassivellaunus and Caesar and might well have ended differently had Harold and his army not just made a forced march from a Yorkshire battlefield; William became the Conqueror only by a whisker.

A hard battle was followed by a harder peace. William's new subjects were belligerent and wily; neither were his own countrymen entirely trustworthy. Potential usurpers seemed to be everywhere, even among his friends and family, but like a clever schoolmaster he kept them busy. Some were given extensive border estates where the Welsh or Scots would occupy their energies. A half-brother, Bishop Odo of Bayeux, was allotted the whole of Kent, keeping him well employed whilst under William's eye; he was always a thorn in the flesh. There were five others; another half-brother, three cousins – distant but demanding – and a step-daughter's husband. William's solution to the problem channelled their ambition and energy, keeping them all within reach for much of the time. Norman nature being what it was, they also kept an eye on each other; the Rapes of Sussex were created largely for them, and were peculiar to that county.

'Rape' was an ancient word, not always referring to violent crime. In this instance it came from an Icelandic word for the long rope once used to indicate a demarcation between areas of land. It is still in use at Bosham Quay, that Sussex paradise for yachtsmen where an ancient wooden building still serves as a store for ropes and tackle – The Raptackle. William divided Sussex into six rapes; six great areas, each running north to south; six ports, six forests, six principal markets, six roads to London (remember all the Roman spadework), six suitable sites for castles and six useful rivers.

A very distant cousin, Roger de Montgomery was perhaps the least to be feared. At Hastings he had fought valiantly beside William, and he was made tenant-in-chief of two Rapes, Chichester and Arundel, leaving one apiece for the others.

As tenants-in-chief, all five noblemen were expected to keep trade up and rebellion down. They had communication by river and road, and trade via sea ports and inland markets. There were as yet no castles, which to the Norman mind were essential; they must be erected in each Rape as soon as possible. Lesser forts were also needed where the countryside was hospitable to bands of rebels and robbers. There was plenty of work for everyone. Making doubly sure, each noble had estates in other parts of the realm, needing still more time and energy. William's friends and relations were caught in a glittering web; unable to refuse wealth and power, they and much of their property were within reach of his sword arm. Thanks to the Rapes, his Sussex roads and ports, essential for communication with his Continental domains, were maintained at little cost to himself; the indigenous population, similarly, was under surveillance.

When out of earshot his subjects, whether Saxon or Norman, referred to him as William the Bastard. This was due basically to natural causes, but it relieved many pent-up emotions – though his genius and courage seem admirable at this distance. Such a stigma was a heavy burden at that time and he felt it deeply, yet he rose above it to rule with vision and strength.

The Raptackle, Bosham: a storehouse for yachtsmen's ropes and tackle

Each Rape was named after its chief town: Chichester, Arundel, Bramber, Lewes, Pevensey and Hastings. Then, each town was also a port with safe anchorage; not so today, for the coastline has changed. It is curious: one is accustomed to the notion of heavy seas pounding great cliffs to sand, advancing steadily inland, inch by inch, century by century; in fact, the reverse has happened along parts of the Sussex coast. In searching for William's ports and harbours, the modern traveller may find the right location, but he could well park his car in the place where Norman ships rode at anchor. Then, the sea came in a wide estuary to the foot of the hill on which stand the ruins of Bramber Castle; ocean-going ships could anchor and deal with cargoes. The estuary was so wide that a bridge about fifty-seven yards long was necessary to connect the castle with neighbouring Beeding village. Now, Bramber is at least four miles inland and busy with cars. Where William gazed from his wood-patched fort at Pevensey, facing the chill sea winds, today's visitor stands in that very same fort looking across farmland. Laden ships once came along the Ouse to the port

Bramber Castle – the admonitory finger

of Lewes, principal town of East Sussex. It now stands five miles inland. Hastings Castle, high upon a rock jutting out to sea, protected its harbour. Now, it overlooks part of the town. Chichester was a sheltered port; Arundel, of increasing importance as Montgomery's castle progressed, was served by the Arun, navigable by larger ships as far as Ford, and thereafter by smaller vessels to the town itself.

To build Arundel, and each of the other great castles, took many years, but William needed numerous visible signs of his authority, and quickly: instant castles. One of his first acts on landing at Pevensey was to send Odo along to Hastings to supervise the construction of the first. Less dramatic than great stone towers, the instant variety are still common in Sussex, correctly known as motte-and-bailey castles, consisting of a large central mound of earth (the motte) beside a level area (the bailey) all surrounded by a moat or ditch. There were individual variations according to local needs, but the basic edifice was comparatively simple. Indeed, it was even more simple if one of the prehistoric hill forts happened to be handy; half the work was done already. Curved mounds, oval or round, their foundations reinforced by the passage of a few thousand years; they were ideal, ready-made mottes, saving much time and organization. Castles were Topsy-like creations always depending upon current requirements – prehistoric, Saxon, Roman, Norman *et al.* – they 'just growed', and many remain as landmarks.

Pevensey Castle is perhaps foremost in the Topsy class. The Romans built their fort on that site to repel Saxon attacks, and it would be strange indeed if later Saxons ignored its possibilities when Danish longboats used the area as a convenient lay-by, during their forays along the Channel. William of Normandy made excellent use of it, and when the Rapes were organized, Robert, Count of Mortain, repaired the old Roman walls and erected a massive keep within them – a suitable occupation for Odo's brother. It was not until the 1939 war that Topsy of Pevensey received the finishing touches. The countryside had been hastily scattered with brick or concrete pillboxes – tiny defence stations from which marksmen could peep through narrow horizontal slits, and pick off advancing invaders. In those early, desperate days many strange things were devised for the defence of an apparently defenceless realm. Some inspired official in that Sussex fast lane noticed the vertical slits in the Norman towers at Pevensey, built by Count Robert of Mortain for the use of his tall archers with their longbows. So it happened that sundry discreet additions were made to Count Robert's work – additions well in the romantic tradition of made-to-measure ruins, and blending perfectly with the ancient work. Surely no one but Pevensey's oldest inhabitant would notice that anything other than Norman work stood on Count Robert's site...

Except that the ruined keep had acquired sundry horizontal slits for missiles other than arrows. They remain, youthful additions, not yet half a century old, yet blending into that castle, as much a part of it as the Roman masonry.

Motte-and-bailey castles were the antithesis of this lengthy development. They had living-space; the bailey, defended by a ditch, a bank, or a moat – whatever could most easily be installed – was a flat area with space for everyday buildings. The motte, similarly defended, was the safer eminence to which inmates could retreat if attacked. Wood was the usual material for buildings and palisades – wood from the forests which then covered great areas of each Rape. With material and labour available on demand, and the main portion of the work often prefabricated by long-departed generations, they were ideal; impressive enough to stand as centres of authority until the great castles were complete, and durable enough to remain as such in places where a larger edifice was unnecessary.

Bramber Castle began in this way, on a prehistoric mound, most conveniently placed to overlook all the activity on the quay beside that busy estuary. William de Braose, holder of Bramber Rape, also held other more distant estates; the instant castle was essential, but he set about building the real thing as soon as possible. Authority must be represented by massive masonry.

It still is. Though most of the stonework has disappeared, the ancient mound still supports some remnants; most noticeably, part of a tower – one admonitory finger standing alone, not on the summit but pointing high, and visible from the surrounding countryside. If ever there were sermons in stone, Bramber has one in that finger: 'Behave yourselves, or else...'

Descendants of William of Normandy found that sundry magnates, perhaps not quite in the baronial stream of society, were turning their manor houses into pseudo-castles by crenellating the roof, adding the military to the residential, with unacceptable possibilities. The Bastard's brood dealt with that. Crenellated houses must be decrenellated unless planning permission had been granted. Officially it was known as 'Licence to Crenellate', but it meant much the same then as now: impotent rage.

There is a general conception of castles as centres of imposed discipline and regimentation from which came forth warriors, riding or marching, and flying animosity in the form of arrows or molten lead. Alternatively they were stark fortresses withstanding fierce and repeated onslaughts. Many indeed fulfilled such roles. Winchelsea and Rye suffered terribly from French attacks, for in medieval days they were the first line of defence, right on the coastline. Lewes also suffered.

Others more fortunate have stood for centuries, seemingly indestructible and romantic, rising like Excalibur from lily-strewn lakes and moats – Bodiam and Herstmonceux, neither of which has ever seen hostilities. Both are moated, but so extensively that each seems to rise from the bed of a great lake; memorable indeed. Sussex has many beautiful landmarks; these are surely among the loveliest. They have grace, peace and majesty, and all these things are as secure as such things may be in this world. In the Civil Wars Bodiam was fortunate: purchased by a Parliamentarian, it was slighted only from the inside, so that the outer beauty remained to attract an eighteenth-century saviour. In our own century it was completely restored to its present beauty by Lord Curzon, who then bequeathed it to the National Trust; a superb gift. Herstmonceux and its grounds became the home of the Royal Observatory in 1948 – surely a most unusual location for a scientific institution. When seen as part of the Observatory's history of more than three centuries, the near-forty years at Herstmonceux seem little more than a bed and breakfast stop-over, and that may soon be terminated.

The Royal Greenwich Observatory was transferred from its original home in Greenwich Park when London air became too heavily polluted; everything was moved to Herstmonceux. Extra buildings were erected in the grounds, including domes and the great telescope. Very little of the castle was left open to

Beautiful Bodiam: even the Puritans were reluctant to damage it

visitors; even so, the gardens are so exquisite a setting for the castle that visitors still come in great numbers. Those who are of a scientific turn of mind may feel 'so near, so far', for in strolling through those gardens they are as near as possible to one of the most important scientific archives, which is not generally available.

Now, the very latest British-built telescopes are being erected in the Canaries and at Mauna Kea in Hawaii. Herstmonceux will soon be just a castle again.

Only twice in post-medieval days have castle-builders of serious intent left their mark upon Sussex. Henry VIII, having alienated most of Europe, defended the coast from north-east to

south-west with blockhouses. Strangely, Sussex had only one, Camber Castle, built to guard Rye harbour. It was near the shore, with five bastions and a central tower. Four centuries later, it stands well inland, beautifully designed and carefully preserved – a strange memento of such a man. The strangest thing about it is its lack of Sussex companions. There were no cannon-bristling towers to guard Pevensey or Newhaven; Lewes Castle was in ruins, and Chichester Castle had long since been demolished by King John. Camber stood alone in the county. Perhaps the cost had something to do with it. £23,000 was a considerable price, excluding manning and running costs. A heavy price to a monarch who had simultaneously been

Herstmonceux; the ultimate in scientific laboratories

spending money like water, getting into and out of his fourth marriage. Fortunately the expected attack never came.

Napoleon's threatened invasion brought a final rash of single towers, a prime example of the British talent for swift improvisation. Martello Towers were two-storey round towers, tapering a little from about forty feet diameter at the base, the main armament being a 24-pounder swivel gun. There have been two explanations of the origin of these towers; the most usual is splendidly ironic. A tower on Napoleon's island birthplace, Corsica, had recently withstood a fierce attack by British ships, whose officers took note of its details and location: Cap Mortella. The name very soon became anglicized, while the original tower's main features were put to use to defend the Kent and Sussex coasts against Napoleon: Martello Towers.

The alternative story concerns the military architect Horatio Martelli, whose tomb is at Hastings, in St Clement's Church. He died in 1817, after having designed and built such towers – not only for the British but also for the French. A most impartial gentleman.

It is easy to see that both stories may be true, and complementary. Having taken note of that unconquerable tower, what better way for the British to imitate it than to employ the same builder? An Italian, he may have begun merely as a neutral businessman taking the orders as they came; it would seem that ultimately he made his home in England, and no wonder.

The government of the day, unshackled by personal financial involvement as suffered by Henry Tudor, ordered seventy-four towers to guard the coastline from Seaford to Folkestone, each heavily armed. Many still stand; some, merely stumps like old teeth. There are places where the sea has gone into reverse gear and is moving inland, as at Seaford; towers now nearing their second century are unable to take constant pounding unless re-inforced. One is carefully preserved as the centrepiece of a housing estate at Pevensey; another, at Eastbourne, is used as a museum, enticingly known as 'The Wish Tower'.

Towers, blockhouses and castles – all were for protection against human attack, but other round towers were needed for protection against the elements – tides, rocks, currents, mists: lighthouses were essential, but Belle Tout was a mistake. It was

Martello Tower – the fast lane, ready for Napoleon

built by that most well-intentioned of Sussex cranks Mad Jack Fuller, on the top of the headland near Beachy Head. He spared no expense, for he meant it to last; Aberdeen granite was costly and difficult to transport in the early nineteenth century. His great lighthouse stood high on the cliff, with lights so powerful that they could be seen for miles out to sea – except when the mists came down, and they came down frequently.

Though inadequate, it served for many years; from 1831 until the beginning of this century, when the present lighthouse was built at the foot of the cliffs; there, the light was not obliterated by fog. Belle Tout is still above, sturdy as ever, used as a private residence, its odd name still mystifying people, for it has no clear meaning.

Jack Fuller had many things in common with that ubiquitous type the self-made man, except that his wealth, made in iron and the slave trade, was inherited. Rich as he was, he was no social climber; he repeated time and again that he was 'Plain Jack Fuller', no more, no less. He refused a title. In the House of Commons, when the Speaker annoyed him, he became so abusive that he had to be forcibly ejected. He made a virtue of the very common touch.

The pleasure he derived from all his buildings, useful or otherwise (there were plenty of both), must have been at its peak when the great lighthouse was complete. That light would shine for miles out to sea, all was good, all was beautiful. *Tout* was *belle*, named after the cliff on which it stood. Perhaps someone hesitantly murmured that *'tout'* was not grammatically *'belle'*, but a plain man couldn't be expected to remember all the ins and outs of the Frenchies' lingo. He had said it, he had written it, and those who didn't like it could do otherwise. Belle Tout.

Speaking for myself, *tout* is very *belle* a little further along the coastline. Looking across the mouth of the Ouse towards Newhaven, one sees two lighthouses, one each side of the estuary, keeping watch over that busy shipping lane. Twin lighthouses, silhouetted against the glittering water . . . beautiful, in any language.

Another wealthy man at the extreme west of the county had completed his tower some years before Belle Tout. The last Baron Halifax lived at Stansted Park, but he was aware of distress in the outside world. The 1770s were not years of plenty for genuinely plain folk; the most common touch was that of unemployment and starvation. Lord Halifax called in the builders and labourers; he built a high tower at the southern end of a high spur of land on his estate, overlooking Racton Park Wood, and with long views out to sea. £10,000 was a considerable sum, and the construction provided a lifeline for many.

It is often said that this was a folly, and the owner 'fired off guns when he felt like it'. It was most useful, for a folly; ships limping home during the Napoleonic Wars were easily seen from the tower; gunfire alerted the dockyard. Fast signalling would have been essential in the event of any attack; Racton was part of the chain of high places, such as the great beacons of the Downs, from which signals were passed between Whitehall and Portsmouth. It was possible to send a message and return the reply, in

Racton Tower: an eminently reasonable folly

less than one minute. The work of British Telecom is older than one would imagine.

Now, Racton Tower is ruined; the two smaller towers, one each side, have crumbled, but the great central tower stands high enough to be a useful landmark for passing sailors. Travellers driving west from Chichester pass through the village of Funtington and enjoy the picturesque sight from the highest points of the road.

Sussex men with a taste for long views have been well provided for by Nature, at no cost whatsoever. They have those high places on their Downs, great beacons such as Firle and Ditchling, cloud-touching cliffs like Beachy Head and the Seven Sisters – hardly any need for brick-built vantage points.

I always wondered about those Seven Sisters; there seem, just possibly, to be eight. Went Hill, Bailey's Hill . . . Flat Hill? – standing shyly like a small sister . . . Flagstaff Point, Brass Point, Rough Brow, Short Brow, Haven Brow. Take a stroll along the Channel, and see.

It is strange how modest the human race can be, on occasion. The Devil's Dyke, the Devil's Jumps, the Devil's Bumps – all credited to Mephistopheles but due in a greater or lesser degree to human labour. The fact that barrows were burial mounds doubtless brought in the Devil on his sinister waveband – his Jumps, on Treyford Hill, and his Bumps on Bow Hill; but he rode into the dyke on the crest of glorious legend. That it is a combination of natural formation from past millennia topped by a man-made earthwork was no deterrent to folk imagination.

Sussex had become deeply committed to Christianity, with its great abbeys and tiny churches, and the devotion of people high and humble; Satan vowed to inundate the entire county. He would dig a vast channel through the Downs, a dyke which he could breach in an instant, letting in the sea. But even the Devil is subject to rules: his work belonged to the night, and must be completed by daybreak.

St Cuthman found out and duly instructed the sisters in a nearby convent. Every prie-dieu in the chapel was supplied with candles and tinderbox. The sisters knelt to pray. By nightfall the Devil had started digging, and the sisters prayed on in the dark until they heard the first stroke of midnight.

The chapel blazed with light. Every sister at her desk; the lay sisters at the windows – they had candles everywhere; so great an illumination that the cockerels in the convent yard sat up and crowed for so fair a morning. Satan dropped his tools and flew away, leaving behind him the unfinished but magnificent dyke, and many queries about his level of intelligence.

There were other mounds for which no one was given credit; not, apparently, built for burial purposes, but still triumphs of ancient engineering – the Caburn, Cissbury Ring and Bramber.

The most famous is Chanctonbury Ring, a clod of earth which fell from the Devil's spade when he was digging his dyke. It is a mound of many parts, and most people, if asked, would identify it by only one of those parts – that which is not ancient but positively youthful by Sussex standards. Chanctonbury Ring? That great circle of beeches crowning the steep hill near Steyning? But that circle of beeches was the work of a schoolboy, little more than two centuries ago. He was not of the generations required to shape their own future by examination results; his career was pre-planned at his birth. The great house of Wiston, with the estate, was his inheritance. He was expected only to absorb the requisite amount of classical education, possibly make the Grand Tour and take an interest in his property.

For over eighty years Wiston Estate was his great love, and Chanctonbury Hill most of all. Visible from Wiston, it had captured his imagination completely.

> How oft around thy Ring, sweet hill
> A boy, I used to play
> And form my plans to plant thy top
> On some auspicious day . . .

That rounded earthwork at the summit was the perfect place to crown his beloved hill. He also planted seedlings within that circle, not knowing that their stunted growth would, in after years, bring about the discovery of the remains of a Roman temple.

It was a lengthy undertaking. He climbed Chanctonbury with his seedlings, and thereafter daily with water until they were

Chanctonbury Ring: a thing of beauty, and worth a fight

firmly rooted. It is most unlikely that he did it without assistance from the estate staff, but the vision and the achievement are his alone, and he was rewarded beyond his wildest dreams.

> ... And then an almost hopeless wish
> Would creep within my breast,
> Oh! could I live to see thy top
> In all its beauty dress'd.
>
> That time's arrived; I've had my wish
> And lived to eighty-five;
> I'll thank my God who gave such grace
> As long as ere I live.

It sounds idyllic: the privileged boy with a dream; the privileged old gentleman with a dream fulfilled. But what passed in the intervening years? Charles Goring Esq of Wiston had to fight for what he loved so deeply. On 28 September 1786 he drafted a letter; he wrote, crossed out and re-wrote, time and again; it is eloquent of his distress. The final version was sent to Roger Clough Esq at Warminghurst Park.

Sir –

My servant informs me that a great part of my Down with the Ring on Chankbury was yesterday trod in as Part of your Manor and that the turf was dug up in several places as bound marks, and that some other lands in the Parish of Wiston were likewise trod in which I have uninterruptedly enjoyed as part of the Manor of Wiston for which I have a grant with right of free Chace under the Gt Seal of Edward the third . . . I am extremely sorry any matter should arise to cause a Dispute between Families who formerly lived in friendship and good neighbourhood, but the Right in question which is of great consequence to my estates but little to yours, on my part must be defended, so I sincerely hope . . . you will upon fuller information order the Procedures of yesterday to be undone.

Mrs G. sends her compliments to the Ladies . . .

Treading-in, and turf cutting: the oldest of customs to mark land subject to a take-over bid. Roger Clough could have offered to purchase but after long acquaintance with Charles Goring he would have known the strength of the attachment to 'Chankbury'. Those were the days of picturesque estates. With Capability Brown dead only three years since, his ideals were very much to the fore, and the desire to possess Chanctonbury Hill could well rise to an obsession. The beech crown had been growing for twenty-six years; the hill was unique, and infinitely desirable.

Letters went back and forth; on Goring's side, fashioned with great care. Anything that smacked of irritation was scratched out in the draft stage, though some scratchings were deep – the correspondence was an effort. Mrs Goring (the third – Charles' first two wives died early) always sent her compliments to the Clough ladies, and the whole tone was infallibly courteous, though puzzled and pained.

Clough's tone was firm, almost hectoring, accusing Goring of 'hostile measures' in asking for written proof of the claim and claiming his own right from the time of Charles I. Even so, 'Mrs Clough unites with me in best compliments.'

Goring offered a neighbourly meeting at Wiston, but nothing seemed to come of that. One of his last legible remarks was that, 'People are always ready to raise a disturbance between Gentlemen which it is their interest to do so it ought to be ours to avoid the same.' The scratchings are many, and deeper – obviously he was sorely tried, but one cannot tell what then transpired, for the final paper is torn in half and the record ceases.

Eventually, Goring won. His contented poem proves that. 'Chankbury' was his to the end, though at what cost we may never know.

A few miles to the east, the village of Streat was inspired by Chanctonbury when a suitable memento for Queen Victoria's Golden Jubilee, in 1887, was discussed. It was golden in every possible way and, though marked by all the conventional celebrations, something special and unusual was needed. Villagers agreed that a great V for Victoria should be marked in trees, on the high curving downland which overlooked Streat.

Odd tales have grown around that landmark, though it grew to be just as impressive as the villagers hoped. It has been suggested that 'VR' was intended, indicating Victoria Regina, but was abandoned because funds were exhausted. Alternatively, the V was perhaps a later creation to celebrate victory in a later conflict, possibly the Boer War.

However, the year really was 1887. So large a landmark needed many trees; a costly project, but the local gentry, as always (almost) could be relied upon. Mr Lane, Squire of Westmeston, lived only a mile away at Westmeston Place; he paid for the trees on the right side. General Fitzhugh, of Streat Place, paid for those on the left. A well-to-do farmer, Mr Cornwell, supplied the labour. His men brought the trees from Cooksbridge Nursery, which was about ten miles away; a generous contribution even though Marchant's Farm was prosperous. Its workmen did the planting as well, except for one tree on the Streat side. That was put in by Master Cornwell; he was eight years old at the time, but such exciting events were still vivid in his memory during old age.

Responsibility for the Long Man of Wilmington has often been attributed to the monks of the nearby priory. He is only an outline drawing on the slopes of the Downs, but his muscles are now firmly delineated in white concrete, and his height – almost 230 feet – ensures that he dominates the surrounding country-

V for Victoria, exactly as the people of Streat intended

The Long Man of Wilmington: an anonymous artistic achievement

side. It seems unlikely that monks, having abjured the flesh, would have carved out a naked man. True, he is not nearly as naked as the Dorset giant at Cerne Abbas, who posed a dire problem for a Victorian author of a book about hill figures; it was solved by depicting the giant in a primitive leotard which was really no help at all. It is possible that the Wilmington monks drew their Long Man as a reminder that we must leave this world without possessions, as naked as when we entered it, but if so, why is he carrying staves? – very useful possessions to one living on those steep slopes.

It seems more likely that some Sussex man long forgotten had to travel to the chalk Downs of the West Country, and saw the Cerne Abbas giant. He came home and bestowed a more modest figure upon his own locality.

However, when one considers the degree of skill with which the Wilmington figure was drawn, a different thought arises. The artist took account of the effect of the steep slope of the

Downs upon a distant view; he knew about perspective. The Long Man was cut very long indeed and must have seemed quite disproportionate to the labourers who cut the turf. Viewed as intended, from afar, he is stocky but perfectly proportioned. One is immediately reminded of that earliest triumph of the hill artist's art; Uffington Horse, in Berkshire. Deft lines, cut as trenches, create the impression of a leaping thoroughbred which, to this day, no artist could hope to surpass. Surely the Long Man was either an early specimen of the work of that same genius, or at least the work of a talented disciple.

There is another landmark on a hillside near the Long Man; a little horse cut in the chalk on High And Over Hill. Its origins, and those of its predecessor which was nearby, have caused much doubt and discussion.

One local family named Ade was concerned in the making of both, though the date of the first seems uncertain; one tradition suggests 1838, in celebration of Queen Victoria's coronation, but the family records seem to have no definite confirmation.

The first horse was cut when a party of youngsters, mostly farmers' sons, went by boat from Alfriston to High And Over for a picnic. James Pagden and his brothers, from Frogfirle, with a young cousin, William Ade of Milton Court Farm, enjoyed their day; cutting the horse was a sudden whim. Many hands made light work with startling speed and durability – the horse was still visible at the close of the century. After that, deterioration was more rapid, due mainly to the immense rabbit population.

In 1924 John Ade walked on High And Over with Mr Bovis, one of his farm workers who was a kindred spirit. 'What can we do to startle the natives?' 'What can we do to die famous?' – they shared an impish sense of humour. John knew where the old horse had been, though nothing remained. William Ade had helped to cut that – why not cause a sensation with another? Not appearing in one afternoon, but better still, overnight?

> He had at home a picture of a famous horse which he much admired and took it for copy. He drew a plan and made careful measurement and I made many wooden pegs and took a new ball of binder twine and two new wagon ropes for outline to dig by. . . . We must bear in mind it had got to look

'What shall we do to startle the natives?'

right from a mile or more across the Cuckmere valley, and a man standing digging on the side of that hill in the middle of the night was liable to get out of true. After trial and error we were satisfied and conspired with another member, one Eric Hobbis. . . . We chose our full moon, cold and frosty, and arrived about 7 p.m. and hid the car in the bushes, devoutly hoping there would not be any night spooners come poking along. Luck was with us and our pegs and pattern fell into place nicely and so we dug and cast the soil as far as we could to leave a clear bottom outline. We finished about 5 a.m. and I got home just in time to sit down and milk some cows . . .

It was a good night's work. Not until 1949 did the horse need renovation; Eric Hobbis had left the district, but John Ade and his friend Bovis found another helper of like mind, a builder's merchant called Harris. There was a second enjoyable nocturnal expedition for three.

James Pagden's daughter Florence explained the first little horse in her book *The History of Alfriston* published in about 1899. John Ade's sister and sister-in-law, with the help of Mr

Bovis, explained the second in the magazine *Sussex Life*. Even so, the mystery stuck, almost as if people preferred it that way.

Lewes has a strange public house. Outwardly, it is normal; the name is unusual, but the ubiquitous variety such as 'The King's Head' or 'The Rose and Crown' are not mandatory. 'The Snowdrop' is surprising but permissible. More surprising is the fact that this open house of friendliness and comfort will, as long as it stands, be a memorial to a tragedy; a very curious tragedy. Who would expect, in Sussex, an avalanche of devastating proportions?

Christmas week in 1836 brought a heavier snowfall than even the oldest inhabitants could remember. All through the weekend it fell, and a gale swept it into great drifts, some as deep as twenty feet. Lewes was cut off, except by the river. The *Sussex Weekly Advertiser* gave an account:

> It was observed on Monday that the violence of the gale on the previous night had deposited a continuous ridge of snow, from 10–15 feet in thickness, along the brow of that abrupt and almost perpendicular height which is based by South Street and the Eastbourne road, where tons upon tons seemed to hang in a delicately turned wreath as lightsome as a feather, but which, in fact, bowed down by its own weight, threatened destruction to everything beneath. Considerable fears were entertained on Monday for the safety of that line of houses immediately under the hill known as Boulder Row, and these apprehensions were not diminished when, on the eve of that day, a considerable fall occurred at Mr Wille's timber yard which destroyed a sawing shed and forced it from its position upwards of forty feet.

The owner of the yard warned those of his labourers who lived in Boulder Row to go at once to rescue their belongings, but they refused. By the next morning the overhanging snow had developed great fissures, and the cottagers were again warned and offered accommodation elsewhere, but still they refused.

Onlookers were becoming desperate; by a quarter past ten, two young men rushed into a couple of cottages and tried to drag out the women, still without success; hardly were the men clear again before the great wall of snow slid down, crushing and burying seven houses. A gentleman watched in horror:

> '. . . a scene of the most awful grandeur. The mass appeared to strike the houses first at the base, heaving them upwards; then breaking over them like a gigantic wave to dash them bodily into the road; and when the mist of snow which then enveloped the spot, cleared off, not a vestige of habitation was to be seen – there was nothing but an enormous mound of pure white. . . .'

United in horror, everyone struggled; with spades and hands, labourers and gentlemen together – it was a mighty effort. There were six survivors, including Mary Taylor's baby, shielded by her body. The baby was only bruised; Mary, wife of John Taylor, left ten other children motherless. Eight people died, that Christmas Eve, from an old man of eighty-five to a little girl of eleven. And the Snowdrop Inn stands, a reminder and landmark extraordinary.

So great a tragedy – fortunately unique; but this beautiful county has equally unexpected pleasures. Think of mountaineering. Certainly Sussex has great heights, but only on the Downs, where it is walking country. The most mountainous landmarks are surely the great coastal cliffs, Seven-or-Eight Sisters and Beachy Head, none of them suitable terrain for aspiring mountaineers.

Travel north-east, where the forests of the eastern Rapes – Lewes, Pevensey and Hastings – grew densely enough to provide timber for William's vast building needs, and excellent hunting to keep the hyperactive barons happy. Here, Sussex changes character; at first woodland replaces the Downs. Travellers of sedentary disposition might take a short train journey between Eridge and Groombridge, looking northwards all the way.

The Keep Fit contingent, arriving at Eridge station, might dispense with further transport and take the path to Groombridge, following the track which leads southwards and away through the woods. It may seem a long way, and the going is uneven, but suddenly the scene changes: the woodland ceases and the walkers stand high on the summit of a steep face of sandstone rock, looking down a deep drop to the valley and eventually to the railway.

'... how beautiful the white cliffs stand, along the loveliest shore ...'

From the train, the rocks are impressive, and usually decked with sundry climbers complete with slings, ropes, karabiners – all complete.

In fact, High Rocks, Harrison Rocks or Eridge Rocks – take your choice – are not so high as they appear at first sight, but the valley slopes so steeply from the foot of the rock face to the railway line that they seem far more than their fifty feet.

Some climbers might regret this lack of height, looking upon Eridge as Lilliputian mountaineering. Yet seasoned climbers can enjoy it; these rocks have had many thousand years' exposure to English weather, which has left its mark – many marks. Though a climber cannot climb such great heights as in mountainous country, he still experiences many of the regular difficulties of mountaineering. It is excellent preparation for work on more complex rock faces – no easy option.

Archaeologists have enjoyed Eridge too, finding a great deal of evidence of early occupation. For Prehistoric man, the area was protective: it sheltered him from the cold, and also from predators. But it is doubtful whether it gave him the same pleasure it affords to modern climbers.

2 Postdogs, Ponds, and Other Utilities

Old buildings, ancient landmarks – must curiosities invariably be antique? Think of Crawley New Town – the antithesis, perhaps, of Pevensey Castle, which so slowly developed in fits and starts for more than 1000 years.

Forty years ago Crawley was a little place; too small to be a town, but a medium-sized village. Now, many Sussex folk watch it with trepidation. It has not 'just growed'. Rather, it has been forced like rhubarb; fertilized, grafted, expanded – the term may vary but the trepidation remains. Will it absorb any more of the surrounding countryside? England has never adjusted to cold-blooded conurbation; it is too closely reminiscent of that wretched planning permission invented by the Bastard's Brood. Un-British.

In the midst of a county so rich in things of ancient times and gentle evolution, here is a town, grown to order; forty years' growth grafted on to an amalgamation of Ifield, Crawley, and Three Bridges. A patched-up job, some would say, though it was done with the very best intentions – the provision of homes and employment. Many people live happily there; the planners did their utmost and have not been entirely unappreciated, un-British though their activities may have seemed.

Cooked-to-a-recipe Crawley; a curiosity in itself. Yet within that modern curiosity there lurks another *par excellence*, as British as they come; a branch of the Civil Service. The Paymaster General's Office.

Outwardly, it looks normal – for Crawley. It is housed in a large modern building like a pile of boxes stuck together. Local residents know it as Alcatraz. Inside, the staff are not numerous but they work with an accuracy and promptitude which could not be excelled even by Herstmonceux or the coming glories of Hawaii. They manage to harness all the virtues and none of the vices of that dubious mod con, the computer, but perhaps computers accepted for service with Her Majesty's Paymaster General know their place.

POSTDOGS, PONDS, AND OTHER UTILITIES

Thoroughly modern, and efficient to match; but even so, a curiosity, for this is one of the better brainchildren of Henry VIII. It is not quite 500 years old, but fits into its twentieth-century surroundings without a trace of Olde England.

That monarch was a master of the art of delegation. Anything you could do, he could do better, but that never deterred him from avoiding the labour whilst retaining the pleasures of criticism. He needed someone to deal with the expenses of specific military expeditions, and for many years it was a one-man job. A Paymaster was appointed, and a lump sum was handed over for disbursement at his own discretion. Often, discretion was an elastic term; indeed, the position was for a long time regarded as a legitimate form of self-enrichment. There were very few Paymasters who paid out rather than paid in: it was not until the eighteenth century that complete integrity came to the appointment when the elder Pitt took over. It was high time, for by then the responsibilities had expanded far beyond the salaries and expenses of the armed forces, and included pensions. Now, the Paymaster deals not only with the armed forces but with pensions for the Civil Service, National Health Service, and teachers.

The office had always been based in London until an air raid brought a direct hit; the department came to Crawley, and stayed. Henry VIII's brainchild, matured and perfected almost beyond recognition from its Tudor days had become of the most important entities in Crawley New Town.

The Paymaster General now sends his little benedictions by post. If the department so improved by Pitt had adopted that method before 1849, they might, in Sussex, have been delivered by a team of dogs. Post was delivered in this way, at least between Steyning and Storrington, until that year, when the public highways were considered far too busy for the continued use of 'draught dogs' and it was made illegal. But in Steyning, next to Springwells Hotel, there is still Dog Lane where the teams were kennelled. They probably had a much better life than strays.

Near to Springwell House, between two and three centuries ago, there were 'certain wells called Singwells'. One was holy, and therefore covered with a shingled roof, like many churches. Shingled Well . . . Singwell . . . Springwell.

Dog Lane, where draught dogs rested between postal deliveries

Wells and ponds – so important to country life; in Sussex, ponds existed in three different varieties. Village ponds, hammer ponds, and dew ponds. Village ponds were all-purpose things: for the ducks, dogs and firefighting; for carters to wash clogging mud from their wheels in winter – Sussex roads were proverbially terrible; and even more important, for them to soak their wheels during a hot dry summer. Long dusty days on the roads dehydrated the wooden wheels, shrinking them away from the iron rims. A soak in the village pond repaired the damage.

The term 'hammer pond' is a misnomer; 'hammer lake' would be better. These great stretches of water, beautiful and peaceful now, were first created some 500 years ago to make waterpower strong enough to forge iron. Watermills had long been used for the comparatively simple process of grinding corn between millstones; now, it was possible to make enough power to work the machinery of blast furnaces and forges. The process appeared in England near the close of the fifteenth century, just as the Tudor dynasty was establishing itself. The old method

Chithurst Hammer Pond: power station extraordinary

layered the metal between charcoal which was kept alight by small, primitive bellows. It took several days to make the iron workable, and left too much waste, even though iron was plentiful in Sussex.

To create enough water-power, numerous brooks were diverted to run together, forming large lakes. The power was tremendous, driving mammoth bellows and hammers with a force which would be breathtaking even today, if it were restarted. Strange, that such force, in those days, seems never to have aroused any suspicion of witchcraft. Church and State, abbey, palace and battlefield alike – all used the products of the mighty forges, and the ironmasters grew vastly wealthy. Now, Sussex has many smooth lakes like that at Leonardslee; not a ripple on the silver surface, each one a haven for water birds and a mirror for dragonflies, and a source of astonishment for people meeting these strangely named but lovely lakes for the first time.

Dew ponds were centres of peace, not power, but they also were misnamed. They are certainly ponds, but the connection with dew is tenuous at best. Shepherds called them sheep ponds; shippons. High on the Downs, they watered the great flocks of sheep which grazed there. The pasture was ideal, but having climbed so high, the animals needed water, especially in hot weather. To carry it to such heights up those steep slopes was impossible, but dew ponds offered a solution.

They were man-made. Shepherds noticed that when heavy mist drifted away from the heights, pockets remained a little longer in rounded natural hollows like dimples on the face of those great hills. There, a dew pond could be made. If there was no hollow in a place where a pond was needed, one could be made.

Ponds must be made with care, or the water would soak away through the permeable ground beneath. There were many different ways of dealing with the problem. The simplest was to puddle the surface: it was rammed and hammered until it bonded, smooth and glossy. Had it been allowed to dry out, it would have become crumbly and permeable again, so the pond was 'started off' with a small quantity of water; this preserved the puddled surface until rain and mist filled the hollow.

A Sussex man, Edward Martin, had been filled with curiosity about dew ponds since his schooldays, about a hundred years ago. Being told by an authoritative adult that dew ponds were replenished entirely by dew, he wondered (*sotto voce*, in those days) what became of the rain which presumably fell in and around.

There were other interests in his life, but this became so strong that in later years the Royal Society made him a grant to enable him to study dew ponds for three years. He tramped, climbed, counted, measured and experimented, concluding that dew had no appreciable part in filling the ponds; the heavy downland mists, which could saturate the thickest overcoat in minutes, performed that task with the help of the rain.

Martin listed over thirty dew ponds in Sussex, but four were made of cement or concrete – not the real thing though serving the same purpose. All but one were circular; the reason for a rectangular specimen at Plumpton never materialized. Some were small; Shambledean was seventy-seven feet round. Others were larger according to need, as at Stanmer Down, where the dew pond was 112 feet in circumference.

Methods of construction varied widely; some experts began very deeply, as much as six feet down, with clay puddling. A thick lining of straw was laid on that, followed by chalk puddling. Finally, a sprinkling of chalk rubble or rough stones discouraged the sheep from perforating the chalk surface with their sharp hooves. Other pond-makers worked in less complicated fashion, relying on simple clay or chalk puddling. Much depended upon the tradition prevalent in family, farm or district. Everything depended upon the position of the pond: it must essentially be close to the summit of the Downs, open to the heavy moisture from those impenetrable mists, and ready to receive all possible rainfall. The shepherd was the man who knew; to him, they were sheep ponds or mist ponds. 'Dew pond' was an irrelevant romanticism.

The name was variable, also the method of construction. So was the cost. Made by one of the teams of experts who travelled the countryside, a pond might cost as much as £300. Alternatively, one of the simple chalk-puddle ponds using a natural hollow could cost little more than muscular fatigue. Whatever the cost, a carefully constructed pond would probably last for about a hundred years.

Some still remain; neat oases, reminders of the times when

Chanctonbury Dew Pond – the shepherds' mist pond, or shippon

Sussex Downs were entirely sheep land. Steep slopes which defied the plough in pre-tractor days have now been changed from sheep pasture to crops. Water, which had to be gathered from wells, mists and rain, is now harnessed and delivered by electricity, pumped high or low according to requirement. Dew ponds, like hammer ponds, rest in silence.

In 1896, they were searching for water at Heathfield railway station. The London, Brighton & South Coast Railway travelled through very hilly country, and the route was necessarily very winding. Steam-engines needed lavish supplies of water, and the sump at the north end of the down platform, though seventy-three feet deep, did not collect enough. The Company decided to bore much further; water must be there. They went to over 300 feet, but there was nothing – just a very bad smell. The atmosphere was over-anxious; someone lit his pipe, and laughingly tossed the match to the top of the tube.

It was a lucky day. A great flame burst out, but no one was near enough to be injured.

At Heathfield station now, all is quiet. Trains no longer run; traces of the lines are only just visible. The station building has been converted to a pleasant dwelling. There is nothing to show that at one time the whole station and numerous houses in the vicinity were serviced by Heathfield Natural Gas; that more of the gas, transferred to cylinders, was sold for use in other parts of the country; still less, that there were confident expectations that Heathfield would eventually rival Pittsburg, the great industrial city of North America where over 400 factories and 7,000 dwellings were supplied by local gas.

It all began without ostentation. They were looking for water and found none. Gas was a bit of a nuisance. It had popped up in the 1870s when they were boring during the Subwealden Exploration. Here it was again – luckily no one was hurt. As before, they took out the bore tubes and left everything tidy: nothing else would have happened had the Press not found out. There were questions. Most of London was lit by gas – why did the Railway Company not light Heathfield Station with its own free supply? Why was it not providing gas to illuminate all the neighbouring towns?

At the first attempt, pressure was so strong that ordinary incandescent mantles were blown to fragments. A second attempt succeeded, using fish-tail burners, and the station basked in glory. Sightseers came from miles around to look at this great curiosity – a railway station lit by its very own gas. Wider possibilities began to be considered, and a company was formed.

'The Natural Gas Fields of England Ltd' began well, with a qualifying boast that it worked with English capital and English brain. A gas-powered engine (1½ horse-power) was installed to pump water for the steam-engines. Further boring began, and *The Times* was enthusiastic: 'The work is being carried on night and day, and the gas itself supplies both light and power required. In the deepest hole there is a pressure of 200lb to the square inch – more than the working pressure of most locomotives in this country.' It was sufficient pressure to carry the gas to any of the large cities of England; surely there would be enough for them all, for the daily output was already 15 million cubic feet – an eighth of London's daily needs. By 1903 there was much hopeful digging, in and around Heathfield, and the Company even acquired rights to install gas mains along the local railways. Many Heathfield houses were using natural gas.

The optimists were vociferous, yet Sussex natural gas was now largely a matter of drilling and dreaming. Suggestions were wide-ranging. Bring back the glass and iron industries from the North and Midlands; drill to 3,000 feet – at 15 shillings a foot; buy up land to sell as gas-powered industrial sites; American Experience May Be Consulted (forget for a moment the Company's earlier boast about English brain). The pie was forever in the sky, but this was not generally realized. Again, *The Times* was confident:

> ... gaseous fuel might do much less in England than in America [where its production in 1900 was worth nearly £5 million sterling] yet be an important commercial factor. ... It may comfort lovers of English scenery to point out that the success of English natural gas would not necessarily mean the ruin of the sylvan and rural beauties of Sussex. That county was once the seat of a considerable iron industry ... it contains sand of excellent quality for glass making, a manufacture in which gaseous fuel has achieved conspicuous success at Pittsburg. But even should the Sussex gas field fulfil all expectations ... the fuel will be conveyed away to established centres of industry rather than be used on the spot. The casual visitor will scarcely be able to see that Heathfield is different from any other English village. Mr Inverness Watts, the engineer in charge, has devised a plan for constructing the necessary storage underground. ...

Splendid: with one proviso. Profits for the year 1903 (the best) were something under £200. The Company was wound up; so were two others before the end of 1910. The only real use of gas continued in Heathfield, but by 1930 the houses there, formerly using it, had been converted to electricity. The official view was that using the available supply merely to light the station was perhaps wasteful, so it was sent away in cylinders for use elsewhere. It was all very lame compared to those early hopes and claims.

Even as late as 1955, British Petroleum restarted boring at Heathfield, but to no purpose. Esso tried in 1963, though by then even the station's own supply was failing. British Rail's great economy drive was under way, and by 1965 there were neither trains nor gas.

At Heathfield station now, all is very quiet . . .

Go to Arundel, and there you will see a collection of old-style street-lamps. They were made in the days when the lamplighter walked at dusk, carrying a long pole. He put it into the lower vent of each lamp, and using the hook at the tip, he pulled a small lever; the lamp was warmed in golden light. It was not the competent robot flash of electricity; a gas-lamp came more slowly to life. This suited the old town. The warmth, the velvety quality of gaslight suited the nook-and-cranny streets, the old stone, the infinitely varied shop windows – it was all of a piece.

The gas bills were pretty good too. About £2,500 a year for a townful of gas-lamps, in 1968. The change-over to electricity would cost about £20,000 – a heavy bill for so small a town, even taking into account the tourist industry.

Though the change had to be made some time, Arundel decided to attempt to preserve at least the appearance: the gas-lamps would be left in place. It was so long since everyone else changed to electricity that replacing broken lamps was a regular problem, accentuated by a growing fashion among householders for lighting their gateways and drives with antique street-lamps – fitted of course with electricity. Arundel had to buy replacements as and when available, usually singly, or at most in twos – oddments here and there, forgotten items from among other towns' rejects, and from antique dealers.

Then traffic through Arundel became much heavier; in effect, its main streets became main roads. Electricity was essential; the money was found and the change was made.

Then came the bypass.

Skimming the foot of the hill, it avoided Arundel completely; over the river, and eastwards. Arundel's erstwhile main roads were once again main streets. Emotions ran rather too high to be expressed in mere words.

All passion spent, it is now hoped that enough of those Arundel-style lamps may be found, and perhaps they may be modified for use with that expensive but convenient electricity.

On Hastings beach there is another kind of antique which was a foreshadowing of New York.

Towards the end of the sixteenth century, land on Stony Beach was for sale. It was particularly tempting to the local fishermen: close to the sea, a place to make their nets and dry them. Never affluent, their fortunes at that time were very low, and only a few men could buy at all. They bought the smallest plots where there was certainly not space enough to spread out the nets.

Therefore they built upwards, as did the New York builders in later times. The net shops, constructed in heavily tarred wood, are so tall they seem almost to lean together. Among them stands the fishermen's church, though even that has to earn its living, serving as a museum on weekdays and housing a service on Sundays – the same kind of service as would be held at sea.

And when the nets need to dry, they hang from the top of the net shops, dried and freshened by the wind as they would not have been from lower and wider structures. Net shops, or deezes as they are sometimes called – utilities for centuries past; by chance, out of necessity.

Land was dear, money was scarce, so deezes were built

The University of Sussex; the pride of the county

A quarter of a century ago, other buildings began to appear to the east of Brighton. Stanmer Park was a well-known beauty spot, and after many years' discussion it was chosen as the ideal location for the University of Sussex. Not merely red brick, as some scoffers said, but beautiful brick together with modern materials, all used as the basis of a work of art by Sir Basil Spence. No dreaming spires, no pseudo-Gothic, no twee-Tudor; but magnificence, of which Sussex was rightly proud.

In the days when Cambridge was still youthful, still slightly red brick, Oxford was old established and very well endowed, though of course money was always welcome. Cambridge, the adolescent, was in desperate need; it seemed that nothing was forthcoming. A great lady supplied the deficiencies. Lady Margaret, mother of the reigning king, Henry VII, had led a difficult life. Many years passed before her son won the crown at Bosworth; years during which she was often under suspicion, sometimes in danger, and frequently poor, for much of her wealth went to help Henry. Now she was free to give generously to the other cause close to her heart, the Universities; but every pound she gave had been hard earned in endurance and fortitude.

Five hundred years later, though Sussex University was not a voluntary foundation, private contributions were still sought; Sussex people were anxious to be involved in this, their own university.

I studied the list of benefactors. At its head, the very first name brought to mind that great lady of five centuries ago, for here was another great lady. Helena Normanton, QC, one of the first two women in Great Britain to take silk. Think how much the first women to qualify in medicine had to pay in stress and determination, in the face of so much opposition. It was similar, though less publicized, among barristers. To be allowed to qualify, to obtain any briefs, to be able to practise at all; one woman needed the determination of several men to attain the same end. Helena Normanton did so, and was one of the first to reach the top. As with Lady Margaret, every pound she gave had been hard-earned in endurance and fortitude.

Tapsell Gates are few but not far between; all within a ten mile radius of Lewes. They are found at Pyecombe and Kingston-near-Lewes, to the west of the town, and at Friston and East Dean, to the east.

They are unusual in that they move on a central pivot, opening either way; much easier than the normal five-barred gate, particularly the all too common variety with broken hinges.

They stand at the entrance to church grounds, reputedly to enable coffins to be borne more easily into the churchyard, though it seems strange that the gate was not set open beforehand as part of normal preparations.

It is even more strange that so ingenious a design was not copied elsewhere in Sussex, or even, apparently, in other counties. The very localized incidence suggests that perhaps they were the work of one craftsman, or one family of craftsmen.

Considering their principal function, tombstones are utilities, but they also fit into other categories: revelation, communication, works of art, and historical record.

Mad Jack Fuller was known to his contemporaries as 'The Hippopotamus', being considerably oversize in all directions. One wonders how many men were needed to eject him from the House of Commons when he abused the Speaker. He built

An outsize tomb for an outsize man; Mad Jack's pyramid

his own tomb some twenty-four years before he needed it: a pyramid which looks somewhat overblown in the village churchyard, yet entirely appropriate to its occupant. There is a tradition that he asked to be placed within the tomb at a table, with a bottle of wine; a tradition which is usually dismissed as fanciful. Yet it seems to fit the man's character.

Much as he liked to declare himself Plain Jack Fuller, he had a notion of his own consequence. Restriction within a coffin, however carefully made to measure it might be, was a denial of freedom, and that was something all who dealt in the slave trade were particularly insistent upon for themselves. He set out to be idiosyncratic; his buildings were fanciful rather than useful. He lived, as his wealth and forceful personality permitted, according to the whim of the moment, and might well have chosen a similar style within his pyramid. The building is eloquent about its builder.

For a perfect exercise in communication, go to Walberton. A white stone is conspicuous in the churchyard, clean and new. So it appears, among the old lichened and leaning memorials. For those visitors who can read, the lettering is as clear as if cut yesterday.

> In Memory of Charles Cook
> who lost his life
> by the fall of a tree
> 20 March 1767
> Aged 30 years

and alongside:

> In Memory of Sarah
> Relict of Charles Cook
> who died Nov. 26
> 1817

For visitors not so accomplished – a fair number, in 1767 – the whole story is carved beautifully, with the finest detail, as clear as can be. No one could be in any doubt about the tragedy. Charles, greatly distressed, lies beneath a fallen tree, watched by a gentleman in a tricorne hat, who, though concerned, seems to be making no effort to rescue the victim. It would have been useless, for the outcome was pre-determined. Cherubs hover, with trumpets at the ready, and Father Time stands with his scythe, while a skeleton grins from the side of the picture.

Not far from Charles and Sarah lies Lord Woolton, that indomitable Minister of Wartime Food. A great man indeed, but he was not averse to lending a hand when Walberton churchyard needed some tidying.

Other vivid tombstones convey the trade of the deceased, like that of a Lewes carpenter whose tools are all precisely detailed. The loss of an elderly man, dearly loved, is expressed by broken anchors whose chains entwine a stricken tree; not an original image, but perfectly worked.

Revelation or communication, that little memorial tablet in Jevington church? 'Nat. Collier MA, late Rector of this church who dyed Mar: ye first in 169½.' And why not? Neither in 1690 nor in 1691 but somewhere between the two, half-way along. That could have been any time after the end of September; the

Love, grief, and remembrance

years in his time were counted from 25 March until 24 March. Not until 1751 did the government of the day change back to William the Conqueror's arrangement, 1 January until 31 December.

Finely carved stones are of course works of art, costly enough to be out of reach of many people, unless, as sometimes happened, an understanding employer or other benefactor contributed. Yet the desire to commemorate one's departed is no less strong because of a lack of cash. To record permanently the perfections of the deceased, and the undying love of those left behind, helps in some small way to relieve the sense of loss, to fill the void.

Jonathan Harmer, in Heathfield, realized this. He was, among other things, a stonemason of talent. With a family to feed and clothe, he needed several crafts at his fingertips. Bricklaying and land-surveying helped, and when his two sons were old enough they worked beside him; with their mother and four sisters running an economical home, they managed, though the 18th century closed on hard times.

Whilst carving status symbols for the churchyard, he felt sorry for those who mourned in poverty, and turned to mould-making, using the same imagery he used on marble. Veiled figures in graceful draperies, ornate urns full of flowers and fruit, cherubs – clients could choose their design, and then he made a terracotta bas-relief. There was even a choice of colour. Local clay gave a warm, glowing red; clay dug further away from Heathfield produced pale buff or cream.

The memorial plaques were successful. Lovingly crafted, they had no taint of cheap substitution. Those cherubs were made by a man who loved real children. Wing feathers were carefully detailed. Fruit and flowers were formed carefully enough to bring the natural colours to mind.

There was a drawback. As the nineteenth century progressed, times grew harder. Stringent economy in every possible direction was needed, just to pay for a gravestone. The Harmers fully understood. Therefore some stones were erected, engraved and left. Later, a plaque could be chosen and fixed. But even the fixing added a small amount to the bill, and occasionally people would buy a plaque from the Harmer workshop and fix it themselves. So it happens that there is at least one stone remaining on which the plaque has been cemented, but an inexperienced hand, perhaps that of someone unable to read, has covered part of the inscription. Even so, the commemorative urge has been fulfilled.

Tombstones viewed as historical record are sometimes very easy, sometimes very difficult to interpret. Sussex has various monuments showing all the members of a family; boys behind father, girls behind mother, and no one has fidgeted for at least three centuries. The Shelley monument in Clapham church is a gem. Lady Shelley's chin is as square as they come; in the conventional attitude of prayer, she seems to be daring Heaven to cross her. The production of fourteen children under the conditions then prevailing was enough to harden the most gentle of ladies. Sir William is pleading wearily; his judicial garments appear rather limp. Everything is too much for him, and his expression is abject. Upper-class home life is all there, in that monument. The turmoil and expense of children, nurses, servants and a wife of domineering personality; the wife who would be the last to realize that she had fallen into such temptation, and did so simply because of constant anxiety to keep everything running in the manner to which she was accustomed in spite of her all too frequent calls for the midwife. Not a situation exclusive to the olden days.

Other tombstones are more secretive. There is a modest little cross against a half-hidden wall in the grounds of a public school. The inscription is crumbling; the name 'Caroline' is just legible; Caroline, wife of Henry Manning. But Henry Manning was Cardinal Manning, Archbishop of Westminster.

Fortunately, it did not happen all at once. When he married Caroline, he was a young curate working in his first parish; Graffham, Church of England, under her father, John Sargent, the elderly rector. When he died, Manning took his place. It appeared to be the outset of a conventional, comfortable life: Graffham parish church, high on a Sussex hill, tucked in beneath even higher hills; the comfortable rectory down in Lavington; the tiny church there, snuggling beside yet another hill; it was idyllic.

Four years after their marriage, there were rumours that Manning was to be Rural Dean of Midhurst – a significant advance for so young a man. Then Caroline died.

'The little church under a green hillside' – a cardinal's memories

Like so many other people, Manning took a little comfort from memorials. That small cross remains, still showing signs of its original elegance. A stained glass window in the south choir aisle of Chichester Cathedral is dedicated to her. The loss was a heavy blow, but he worked harder than ever, and his family and friends took heart. The friends included Gladstone, who had been a fellow student at Oxford, and Samuel Wilberforce, the brother-in-law who had conducted the wedding four years previously and who eventually became a bishop. Both expected great things from Manning, in spite of his loss. Less than three years after, he was made Archdeacon of Chichester Cathedral.

For a while, no one noticed any setback; then he refused offers of further advancement. Years came and went, and the pensive Archdeacon seemed to desire no further change. No one suspected his real difficulty; when eventually he announced his allegiance to the Roman Church, it broke as a major scandal. Everyone was horrified; his brother disowned him, and in his new role as a Catholic priest he had to start his career from the beginning, all over again. He ought never to have married, and did his best to forget. That Sussex grave mouldered; he did nothing.

As a Roman Catholic, he did plenty; to rise from the lowest of priests to the Archbishopric of Westminster in fourteen years needed concentration, but that was his achievement. While at Westminster, he deferred the building of the new cathedral; he could not bear to put such wealth into a building, even for so great a purpose, when many poor folk lacked the simplest necessities.

Having achieved so much, and having apparently struggled to forget, towards the end he admitted that time, as he once claimed, had not effaced all things: '... the past rises up to me ... the Downs seem to me to be only less beautiful than Heaven ... the little church under a green hillside where the morning and evening prayers, and the music of the English Bible, for seventeen years became part of my soul ...'

In that little church, the celebrant's desk is only a few feet away from the grave marked 'Caroline'. The Cardinal had not forgotten his wife.

There are two memorials which cannot be left out. One stands in the Lewes churchyard of St John sub Castro; it was not erected for the comfort of friends or family; rather, for the comfort of ex-enemies. It was given by Tsar Alexander II some twenty years after the end of the Crimean conflict.

In the mid-nineteenth century, few people understood the reason for the Crimean War; certainly not the soldiers who bore the terrible brunt. Some Russian prisoners were lucky, after a fashion. Forced marches through a Russian winter on starvation diet had taken them to the battlefields. Having survived all that, the prisoners of the British had better food and medical attention than those captured by the French; even then, they had to live through a crowded voyage back to England. To what? They could not have expected anything pleasant – just a chill wait for repatriation. However, on arrival in Lewes, their appearance must have been woebegone in the extreme, and it touched the hearts of the residents. Their welcome was not so much for enemy prisoners, but for returning soldiers unable, as yet, to go home. For the time remaining, Lewes gave them an affectionate home, and there they were as happy as circumstances allowed. Some, losing their resilience at last, died; the very fortunate few

The Russian Memorial: gratitude and friendship from the Tsar

went home. The memorial commemorates those who died in Lewes, mourned by their new friends.

On the Downs above Brighton stands a memorial to Indian soldiers who died of wounds in the 1914–18 war. It was the King's idea to bring Indians to that Palace of Varieties, the Royal Pavilion; the building itself may not have contributed to the peace of mind of true Orientals, but the immensely complicated organization within the hospital certainly did. Hindus, Sikhs and Mohammedans were all patients there, and every difference was carefully catered for, to the extent of providing nine separate kitchens. Visits from the King and Queen and other royalty were frequent, something appreciated by the imperially minded Indians. The hospital saved most of its patients; of the thousands admitted, only thirty-two died. Of those, the Mohammedans were taken to their Mosque at Woking; Hindus and Sikhs were carried to the Downs, where they were cremated upon a high funeral pyre.

After the war, an Indian architect was commissioned to design a memorial to those men. The Chattri Memorial was the outcome, erected on the spot where the original burning-ghat once stood. High on the Downs, its spare beauty expresses true reverence for the memory of '. . . all Indian soldiers who gave their lives for King-Emperor in the Great War . . . in grateful admiration and brotherly affection . . .'.

The Russian, and the Chattri Memorials: not utilities in the normal way, but uncommonly purposeful if regarded as pointers in the direction of peaceful co-existence. Something of a cant phrase, that; until one stands before those monuments.

Now for a secret utility. The workers therein go to work through the woods like the Seven Dwarfs. They dig and blast and pick-and-shovel just like those little fellows, though they are not awaited by Snow White at the end of the day. However, even the Dwarfs lost her to the Prince in the end, so we are all square again.

They were digging for gold. The modern miners are not so glamorous, but their mine is clean and safe. White, in fact. They are mining gypsum. Where they win hands down over the Seven Dwarfs, is in having their very own private road, their own private railway, and a splendid aerial ropeway which swings

The Chattri Memorial – genuinely oriental architecture in Brighto

gypsum through the most secret part of the woods so that scarcely anyone in the outside world knows anything about it.

The private road goes away from the main road and all things commonplace; up and away through the woods, which are almost thick enough to be a forest like Dallington, where William the Conqueror's nobles hunted the boar and directed their woodcutters. The road is long enough and steep enough to lose the idly curious; it leads to the private railway where the wagons disappear into the woodland; now you see them, now you don't. Similarly the ropeway.

Why all the secrecy? Gypsum is no secret weapon. Certainly it is worth a lot of trouble; it is essential material for builders as the basis of all kinds of plaster, and necessary in hospitals, as Plaster of Paris. In general use, it does horse manure a power of good,

and cosmetics would never be the same without it . . . so why the secrecy?

Not why, but where. This activity is all in what is officially termed 'an area of outstanding natural beauty'. The gypsum cannot economically be ignored. If it were not used, costly imports of this essential commodity would have to be substituted. Yet that wooded countryside must not be damaged.

The wooded countryside which created the problem also provides the answer, in the magnificent cover offered by the trees. True, expenses rose fearsomely because the railway and ropeway both had to meander, following the best cover, but that extra outlay preserved both the mine and the countryside. The presence of the mine, though not a State secret, is not widely known. Leave it at that.

3 Man's Inhumanity to Man . . .

Strange, that nasty things should be good for other nasty things; that is to say, bad for other nasty things. A genuine piece of hangman's rope, if twined around the bedpost, ensures safe childbirth. A splinter from a gibbet post is a sure cure for toothache; which is why, if you go to Ditchling Common intent upon seeing Jacob's Post, you will be disappointed. Innumerable toothaches have (presumably) been cured, and when the post was about to collapse the remnants were removed to a public house some distance away. It was a particularly potent gibbet post, for that murder was a triple crime. Jacob Harris killed the landlord of a nearby inn, the landlord's wife, and their maid. Before the landlord died, he managed to raise the alarm and describe Jacob, who was punished in the usual way of the eighteenth century. He was hanged, and his body taken to a spot near the place of the murder; for years it hung in chains from the gibbet. And toothaches came and went.

At one time the post was surrounded by wooden rails, but they disappeared so often for gypsies' firewood that the reeve of the common gave up.

Stocks created the same problem. One Sussex village postmistress was asked by a visitor where the stocks were. She had picture postcards of them on sale, but when she tried to direct the visitor, she could see no stocks. They had been removed overnight – a cold night. Ninfield inhabitants had been wiser, using another Sussex material for stocks and whipping post: iron. Theirs are still in place, as is Harting's wooden specimen beside the church gate. It seems strange to put such things in such a position; certainly, punishment was always a strong point in the Church's teaching – one has only to look at wall paintings for the edification of the illiterate. But the sounds which must have infiltrated so fiercely into the ecclesiastical quiet – the screams, the jeers, the impact of lash and missiles – were surely undesirable.

MAN'S INHUMANITY TO MAN ...

Waiting at the church – Harting's stocks and whipping post

Old Heathfield had stocks, long ago. They stood at the corner opposite the farmery of Heathfield Park, but when they were used to punish an innocent man, the villagers were so angry that they forced the stocks from their base and threw them down the well in the adjoining meadow.

Blind houses, plentiful in the West Country, are less common in Sussex. They are the tiny lock-ups in which two or three prisoners could be shut away for short periods; usually until sober, if drunk; until calm, if belligerent, or until transport arrived if a greater crime destined the culprit for the county gaol. They were convenient for the use of local constables, and so unpleasant that often the threat was a sufficient deterrent. A blind house was so dark that prisoners were, in effect, blind; light was minimal, usually only that which came through the tiny air grille, out of reach. Most were bitterly cold, built with thick stone walls.

Some prisoners used to scrape away the stone around the lock, with varying degrees of success; it depended on the tool – sometimes a button would do. A lucky prisoner would be pushed into the lock-up after his predecessors had done plenty of spade work, though it was all useless if the constable used a padlock. A wooden door might well be rotten and ready for manipulation; repair work was always put off as long as possible.

Northiam lock-up used to be within sight of the church, and one inmate waited until service began. It was hard work, for the wood was still tough, and slow because of the need to be quiet, but gradually be made a space, apparently large enough to squeeze through. The space was smaller and the sermon shorter than he expected; the godly emerged from church in time to catch the ungodly emerging from the blind house.

Most Sussex blind houses have disappeared; events moved more swiftly in the Fast-Lane county. Better communications and more police stations made such half-way houses unnecessary. One very interesting survival has lasted simply because it was not purpose-built. Part of Saddlescombe barn, it was walled off as a makeshift measure – probably early in the eighteenth century. The stone walls were stout enough, but the plank door was an invitation to successive inmates. Several times that door has needed repair, and the farmer had to use anything he had to hand – again as a makeshift measure. His old scythe blades served the purpose well.

One finds the same story in many counties: the lock-up needed repair, money must be spent – but whose? People found the

Saddlescombe blind house: mute witness to generations of ingenious farmers

money to plant trees, build churches or extend great houses; but such non-kudos things as blind houses must be left to someone else – that same body which exists to this very day, known as 'They'. Responsibilities are heaped upon them, from pest-control to making trains run on time and reducing the rates. That much-mended blind house door is strong evidence that some things have changed little, however many years have passed.

Lewes remembers its Protestant martyrs who died rather than become subject to Rome. Little memorial notices meet the eye at numerous points in the town; the war memorial was placed upon the site of some of the executions at the top of School Hill. The pity of it, the waste and the strength of purpose; and so soon after, the valiant response of the Catholics to similar persecution.

One poignant case stands out in the mind. It reaches out from that day to this, for we also live in times when job-creation is necessary. This man was an iron master; the owner of a hammer pond, of bellows and furnace and a great water-driven hammer; a well-to-do man with a strong sense of responsibility towards his family and his workers. He was tried, and sentenced to be burned at the stake. This was his response: 'Let me go home, I pray you, to my wife and children to see them kept, and other poore folk that I would set aworke, by the helpe of God. I have set aworke a hundreth persons ere this, all the yeare together.' They let him go and see to it. Then he returned, as in honour bound, and was taken to execution.

How could it happen, why did it happen? are questions still being asked in the district near Newhaven, still known as Tide Mills. There are no mills, just some battered foundations which fill and empty with the movement of the tides. Sometimes an elderly man walks there who tells the story as though it happened yesterday.

That place was once the site of an unremarkable flourmill until, in the late eighteenth century, it was bought by William Catt. He was a man with a magic touch. Business thrived, and his organization and mechanical inventiveness amounted to genius.

He used water-power: not that of smaller streams harnessed to grind corn; not that of hammer ponds harnessed to drive twenty-foot bellows and half-ton hammers; but the sea itself, and the force of the tides, which was operative here for the greater part of each day. There was power enough for three of the greatest waterwheels ever seen, and one even greater to work the lifting-gear which loaded and unloaded the ships coming into the harbour. Farmers sent their grain along the Ouse; it was ground in the mill and loaded on board. At its peak, this was said to be the biggest flourmill in existence, with a mill building five storeys high; many workers were necessary, and William Catt looked after them. Mostly they lived in the village he built for them; they paid rent – half a crown a week for a cottage; cheap at the price, for their wages were high, and the cottages were well fitted and maintained, as well as being very attractive. Hardly a day passed without at least one painter setting up an easel within

Tide Mills – a self-inflicted wound

sight of them. Those were the days in which back-to-back slums were coming along nicely in other working areas.

'Their' mill, the great mill, was such a masterpiece of engineering that Catt was invited to make a lecture tour of Europe to advise other millers. Though he died in 1853, his work went on for twenty years.

The storm which eventually devastated the mill was greater than anything anyone had ever known. Also, steam-power had become an important rival; caught between storm and steam, Tide Mills could hardly cope. It and its workers limped on until 1884, then finished. The great mill building was dismantled seventeen years later for safety reasons, but the village was still loved and lived in. People might be forced to find other work; the village was permanent, a community of friends, which had been joined in 1924 by a convalescent home for handicapped children. All was well. Then, in 1939, the Second World War commenced.

Perhaps an order had been misread, or misunderstood. Maybe someone in Intelligence received erroneous information of an imminent invasion. We might simply call it an advanced manifestation of the Fast Lane Syndrome. But the Army arrived, gave everybody one whole hour to remove themselves and all their belongings out of range, then blasted the whole village to dust.

Officially, afterwards, it was said that the village might have given cover to the enemy had they landed; there seems to have been no sign even of a threatened approach.

Many thousands of people lost everything – homes, family, possessions and lives – in the subsequent air raids, and the final hideous bombardment by flying bombs. There were also the lonely children, labelled and sent away from home as evacuees; that minority who got into the wrong hands. Hitler was to blame for everything. But Hitler was beaten.

The Tide Mills hurt remains. Inflicted by their own soldiers – there is the rub; and done without any shadow of reason.

Maybe there was indeed a cogent, though on security grounds, inexplicable reason; but over forty years have passed, and if there were any explanation, it might surely be offered. And perhaps that one old man would not feel so great a need to talk over the ancient hurt with strangers.

'It was our own people that did it . . .'

4   ...and Otherwise

Mad Jack Fuller: a familiar name. 'Hippopotamus' was one nickname; 'Mad' was just another, gained through his passion for building follies around his portion of the countryside.

In his day he must have been the equivalent of a millionaire. His father, already wealthy from the iron and slave trades (and a clergyman to boot) married a cousin, heiress to another fortune. The expanding inheritance began in 1777 when Jack's father died. His mother and his uncle soon followed; Mad Jack's fortune was complete. Brightling Park, then known as Rose Hill, and the entire estate were his.

Note the date. Very young men could lose very large fortunes in a variety of ways; debts of honour were frequent. Mad Jack turned elsewhere – perhaps this, in part, was another reason for referring to him as 'Mad'. His interests were scientific and artistic, so that he kept open house for Turner, the painter, and commissioned early works from the then unknown architect Robert Smirke. There was a gift of £10,000 – half a million, nowadays? – to the Royal Institution, and funds to endow two professorships.

He was extravagant nearer home. The village church needed bells – he gave them eight, and they still ring every Sunday. Music was poor during services; he gave a barrel organ, one of those useful cylindrical instruments set to play numerous hymns. They were very popular at the time, and his is still giving good service in an Australian parish. Times had become very hard for ordinary people, so Mad Jack had a long high wall built around his house and park, providing employment for many.

That seems also a likely reason for the smaller follies, apart from the fact that when Smirke designed the Observatory it was with Mad Jack's genuine scientific interest in mind; it was equipped with a comprehensive array of expensive instruments. Churlish, surely, to call that a folly; unlike the Sugar Loaf – a cone-shaped obelisk at Dallington. Mad Jack is said to have made a wager that he could see that unusual church spire from

The great wall of Rose Hill; the method in Mad Jack's madness

Rose Hill. He was wrong, and remedied the error by building a replica, the Sugar Loaf, where it would indeed be visible.

Brightling Needle was his obelisk on Brightling Down, one of the highest points in East Sussex. Presumably, a folly – who needed a landmark when Nature had provided one so superb? But it created employment.

Within his own grounds he ordered a summerhouse, unusual in that he used an artificial stone – Coadware. He may well have designed it himself, for Smirke had not yet returned from abroad, but when he did, a small circular temple was built, also in the grounds of Rose Hill. In later years, Mad Jack's mausoleum, the pyramid, dominated the hushed village churchyard; overblown, alien – but employment for the needy, and very much in Jack's style.

Stories about him tend to be considered apocryphal; a character larger than life attracts all kinds of tales-that-could-have-been-true. He is said to have abused the Speaker in the

Commons – he called him 'an insignificant little fellow in a wig'. But Mad Jack was also a fellow in a wig; he wore one until the end of his life, when they had long been out of fashion. Some say he was put in the Tower for his rudeness; others, that he rode straight home again.

Some say . . . an intriguing theory recently put forward by one of the foremost authorities on Sussex is that those follies were part of a great smuggling enterprise. Mad Jack, with money, personality and intelligence, used the Observatory as a look-out post; it commands wide coastal views. Belle Tout is said to have served the same purpose, though it could have served no purpose at all during those frequent mists. The follies were on smugglers' routes; they were hollow, and the seamen hid the goods there to be collected by the land men. Presumably the follies, being comparatively few in number, were only occasionally used as hiding-places, or the excise men would have had a much simpler task. Yet how does the Needle fit into that theory? The main object was to get the goods away quickly – not to run up the highest Down in the area for a cache that might or might not be there. Perhaps the Needle's role was merely negative – a genuine folly adding weight to the deception about the others.

Mad Jack was in the habit of travelling in a heavily built barouche, carrying pistols and food and attended by at least one outrider, ostensibly as protection against footpads. A man who so fully enjoyed his wealth would not take kindly to the prospect of its being snatched away. Was it also for protection against rival smuggling gangs? It could hardly have been for protection against the excise men. In his social positon as landowner, philanthropist and Member of Parliament, a confrontation with the law would entail the loss of much, if not all he most valued.

There is a plain workaday explanation for his odd mode of travel. He was gross: twenty stone has been the estimate. 'Hippopotamus' was significant. The coach must be heavily built to carry his weight; such a vehicle would stand every chance of getting stuck in deep mud on the proverbially bad Sussex roads, probably more than once in the same journey. There is the authenticated story of a little old lady, her carriage drawn to church by oxen because her horses could not pull it through the morass which passed for a road. Therefore a barouche strong enough to carry Mad Jack would need the outriders' horses to help the four already in the traces – the large gentleman possibly alighted and kept watch with a pistol while the vehicle was freed. A man of that bulk would need a few snacks to fortify himself in such contingencies.

The smuggling theory is plausible and pleasurable. The man was an artist through and through; not at first hand, but he sensed, encouraged and guided the flame in others. That needed money, and smuggling was a common source. His purse was deep but not bottomless, with slavery bringing in a waning income. He spent heavily. Bodiam Castle, that beauty from the fourteenth century, was ripe for demolition when his artistic eye saw through the ruin and the rubble and came to the rescue. A costly venture; was it also a useful station for smugglers? That pyramid in the churchyard stood empty for twenty-four years – or was it otherwise occupied?

I think not. He was, first to last, concerned for the welfare of his people; that is to say, those on the estate and in the surrounding countryside. That, and his innate artistry, made any affinity with gangs like the Hawkhurst mob, who took murder and torture in their stride, unlikely if not impossible. Even his connection with slavery fails to affect the issue; in every age, all but a few are children of their time. His was the age which saw slaves as a different genus – animals in sub-human form. Mad Jack was too concerned with the present to sympathize with those abolitionists who were morally ahead of the period.

Armed travel may have been necessary, not only because of footpads but in case of attack by smugglers resentful of 'Honest Jack' – another nickname, much valued by him, and possibly not bestowed solely because he refused a peerage. If such were the case, that expensive wall served the same protective purpose.

If the follies were indeed built for smuggling, why were they built at all? Surely it would have been wiser to erect a few unobtrusive cottages or farm buildings rather than follies, which were so very obviously his property.

Mad enough and honest enough: both qualities would have been necessary in a man who dared to stand aloof from smugglers when even priests had either to co-operate or to turn a blind eye. Whatever the truth, the follies are curiosities rendered even more curious when viewed in the smuggling context.

When in Ewhurst, look inside the church. It is not unusual to see electric light in a Church of England building, but this is something special; it was fitted in memory of a Methodist minister, and largely paid for by Methodists.

It happened long ago, in the days when Mad Jack was a small boy. John Richardson was the curate at Ewhurst, and as was the custom of the time, the rector, Mr Nairn, left most of the work to his curate. He may have heard stray comments of approval – the young cleric's sincerity, the joyful atmosphere; he took little notice – that was what he paid a curate for.

Then he heard that John Richardson had been seen at John Wesley's meetings after evensong. It was a shocking disloyalty to worship God properly in church and then to stand listening to that dissenting ranter. Who knew what mischief might result?

Immediately, John Richardson was dismissed. Three years of inspired, open-minded work went for nothing. If the young man felt desolate, it was brief, for John Wesley heard and put him in charge of the Foundry Meeting House; there, he very happily stayed. Indeed, the memory of his ministry in both churches was extraordinarily lasting, even well into the twentieth century. The wall plaque explains everything, except that the lighting was so generous a gift: 'The electric light in this Church was installed in memory of John Richardson, Curate of this Parish 1759–1762. He was afterwards one of John Wesley's preachers, and read the service at Wesley's funeral in 1791. He died in 1792 and was interred in Wesley's grave at the City Road Chapel. The entrance of Thy Word giveth light.'

Chichester market cross is a dainty thing. The city has so much that is beautiful: those Roman walls, strong beyond belief; the nearly new theatre (what are twenty-five years between friends?), the sunlit white museum in Little London, the great grey cathedral, the whirligig library, the Roman palace and, like the top tier of the cake, that market cross.

Bishop Storey was a thoughtful man. The year 1500 was not the heyday of creature comforts, but week after week he saw market folk toiling into the city with their produce; farmers, yeomen and cottagers coming to sell, no matter what the weather was like. Such things were part of existence and no one

bothered overmuch, but he saw them standing, soaked and shivering; if rain fell during the long day, it meant a second soaking. In summer, if ever the sun was too strong, shelter was needed again, but not provided. He set to work.

The land cost him £10. The building was costly too, but that seems not to have bothered him. It was octagonal, with buttresses, panels, rosettes, arches, flying buttresses – all the trimmings of a cathedral in miniature. It was for its users 'with free possession, shelter and protection, and freedom from interruption and fines and tolls'. They used it. From time to time there were alterations: a clock was added, a bust of Charles the Martyr, a lantern replacing crumbling upper decorations. It survived centuries of constant use and the hazards of two world wars; the main damage was caused by the weather from which it had protected the people; carving had become blurred by time and weathering.

Recently, it was repaired. Scaffolding boxed in part of the base but tourists still sat comfortably sheltered, transistors playing. High up among the flying buttresses was a very young stonemason, oblivious to all but the feel of the stone; using much the same tools used by Bishop Storey's men nearly five centuries ago; working alone, his rapt expression very likely an echo of theirs. A wonderful inheritance, this market cross, inspiring such delight in those who made and those who remake, and constant pleasure for all who care to stand still and look. A sort of Super Brolly.

Many churches were founded by great families: that of St Philip Howard, in Arundel, comes to mind. Vast and magnificent, it was built and endowed a century ago to commemorate the coming of age of the fifteenth Duke of Norfolk. Others owe their beginnings to saints: one thinks of the connection of Chichester Cathedral with St Wilfrid. But in an East Sussex village there is a church which was the gift of a writer.

Sheila Kaye-Smith became a writer early in life; her first novel was published in her twenty-first year. From childhood she was deeply religious, though attracted by more elaborate ritual than that observed in the church attended by her parents. On her way

To the people of Chichester from Bishop Storey: one market cross

home from school in St Leonards, she often went into Christ Church; it was Anglo-Catholic, and the atmosphere seemed very welcoming – a welcome she accepted as soon as she was able to choose for herself.

Following that first novel she worked on a succession of books, and did not marry until she was thirty-seven. Her husband, the Reverend Theodore Fry, was an Anglo-Catholic priest. After five years, they were both received into the Roman Catholic Church.

Looking for a peaceful home in which to work, they bought Little Doucegrove near Brede. It was a typical purchase for people with such requirements: a large barn for conversion, with a ruined oast-house and fifty acres of overgrown land. They seemed to be all set for seclusion.

The Frys were of course able to go to Mass by car; it was a considerable journey, but no hardship. Then, they found that there were other Roman Catholics in the area, less well off, who were unable to attend Mass, having no transport.

There was a spacious loft in the old stable building. It was cleaned, repaired and converted into an oratory. Their priest agreed to take a monthly Mass, and the Frys bought a van to transport those Catholics who were too elderly or still too far away to walk. It was Sheila's happy thought to name the Oratory 'The Upper Room'.

So much for seclusion. This arrangement was deeply appreciated by more and more people; soon the priest was saying Mass every week. Sheila took on the main parish work of sick-visiting and teaching children the catechism.

As the congregation grew, so did the quantity of death-watch beetle in the floor of the Upper Room. Some of those fifty acres were going to be useful; architects and surveyors were called in.

Just five years after that first Mass in the Upper Room, a new church was opened; the gift, from the Frys, of the Church of St Thérèse of Lisieux.

Glyndebourne, one of the most famous opera houses in the world, was the creation and gift of a physics master. On a miniature scale, it was created within a minor stately home which had belonged to the same family for 400 years. The period had not yet arrived in which such homes, in order to survive,

To fellow Catholics from Sheila Kaye-Smith — the Church of St Thérèse

were forced to admit the public, yet in 1934 Glyndebourne's owner opened the doors — not with the object of making money, but in the full expectation of losing it.

John Christie had been the only child of a wealthy but broken home. By conventional assumptions he might therefore have been spoilt as an only child, neurotic from his broken home, and arrogant, considering his great family wealth and the fact that his mother was an earl's daughter. Not so.

After Eton, he spent a reluctant year at Woolwich as a prospective army officer; a fortunate accident enabled him to leave and take his degree at Cambridge, returning to Eton as a physics master. That the accident left him lame for life seemed a small price to pay. Another accident seriously reduced the sight of one eye. When the Great War began, the young man accustomed to the academic life of his choice, with a private income and a salary to add to his comfort, enlisted immediately for active service. Briefly, he managed not to limp; when his eyes were tested, he diverted the attention of the MO and covered the damaged one twice. He was accepted, and proved to be a good officer.

'No stretchers – it was light before I could get my last wounded away... I had promised them I would not leave before they did.'

Another officer wrote home of horrors defying description, then – 'Christie was absolutely calm... at one time he stood on the edge of the crater to see what calibre the shells were... sitting in the battered trenches under the same relentless shell fire he produced "The Faery Queen" (sic) and read it aloud to cheer us up.'

He found his name on a list of recommendations for the DSO and crossed it off, but a subsequent Military Cross managed to stick. One would have thought that in earning two decorations and receiving one, Christie had proved himself useful, but his old disabilities were discovered and he was invalided out.

By the autumn of 1916 he was back at Eton, but weekends were spent at Glyndebourne, one of the family estates. It would not legally be his for another four years, but his grandfather had given him full responsibility. The house, mainly Victorian, was large; built more for spaciousness than comfort, it covered most of the remnants of smaller houses which had been on that site for 500 years. Christie disapproved. Ugly furniture, bad pictures, a useless fives court; some of the later additions must go in favour of better kitchens; there must be bathrooms, electric light – and an organ room.

His mother was more economically minded, and horrified, but he insisted. One of his old friends at Eton, Dr Lloyd, had been organist at the Chapel Royal, and through that friendship Christie's love of music had grown tremendously. Lloyd was due to retire and would live near Glyndebourne; money-raising recitals would be useful – good causes were proliferating. Just before the organ and its room were completed, Lloyd died. John Christie pressed on with the project. 'It will be a source of great intellectual pleasure to me for the rest of my life, and to many others.'

Many others; they were returning from the war, many terribly disabled, and vast numbers with no employment in prospect. Christie was concerned. There was plenty of room on the estate, and he set to work to start businesses: Glyndebourne Motor

Works; Ringmer Building Works; a timber works in his own woods; the home farm, employing twenty-six men; and the gardeners, headed by a man who, having been taken on after the briefest of interviews, was to make the Glyndebourne gardens second only to the opera as an attraction.

There were almost a hundred employees, and Christie knew them all. Many stayed for years, for the jobs were never stop-gap work. Such a multiplicity of interests kept the owner fully occupied, and he resigned from Eton, though he enjoyed the company of friends at weekend parties, and they brought other contacts. A well-to-do family was looking for a holiday home during the summer vacation, and they were accepted as paying guests at Glyndebourne. John and Fanny Mounsey, both able pianists, brought their four children, and the friendship blossomed. One of their greatest interests was opera; with them, Christie travelled to Italy and Bayreuth, and they so enjoyed each other's company that arrangements were made to use Glyndebourne as a permanent Mounsey home. John Mounsey, a director of Barclay's Bank, also ran Barclay's staff choir; Fanny was soon immersed in Sussex musical life. At last the Glyndebourne organ was useful, accompanying the operatic performances she arranged; at first, concert versions; later, they were performed in costume. It was an attractive venture even at that early stage; by 1928 there were regular Sunday concerts, not all operatic but all well attended – a happy and satisfying period.

It was cut short by John Mounsey's sudden death. Fanny withdrew with her children to London. For over a year John Christie lost interest in music and in Glyndebourne, and moved into a cottage. He needed time. Death in the trenches was a constant cruelty which he would never forget; this sudden loss, in the midst of happiness, was harder to bear. When at last he returned to Glyndebourne, he wondered whether perhaps it might help to put on just an excerpt from *Meistersinger* at Christmas.

His usual singers declined the invitation but suggested that the Carl Rosa Company might help. They were the only touring opera company, travelling around Britian, living hand to mouth but working to a high standard, rather like a repertory theatre – 50 shillings a week, nothing found but fares and costumes.

The offer of 5 guineas each, plus Christmas board and lodging in a country house, and all for just one performance, seemed magical to two of the company, a tenor, and a young soprano, Audrey Mildmay.

In a way, she was the girl next door. Her father, a clergyman and heir to the Mildmay baronetcy, had had a Canadian living during her childhood. Since their return to Britain she had studied music and toured with the Carl Rosa Company. Her father was incumbent at Herstmonceux, scarcely ten or fifteen minutes' drive from Glyndebourne – judged by John Christie's driving.

He, at forty-seven, had found his ideal: delightful, restful, very pretty – not a great singer but a very good one. He was radiant and gave her no peace; presents and letters followed the Carl Rosa Company everywhere. It took him less than six months; they had a quiet wedding, with Childs, his butler, as best man.

The honeymoon was enlivened by an appendectomy apiece; perhaps inspiration came in the drowsy post-operative stage; Glyndebourne, plus Audrey; of course – an opera house. Just a small one.

Opera houses take time and trouble; plans, designs, working out possibilities – it would be expensive, but that was unimportant. Audrey, used to the real thing, wanted to know why he couldn't do the thing properly.

That seemed to make sense. Glyndebourne Festival Opera was on its way.

From the first, it was a curiosity. To some, the British Bayreuth; to others, a fool's notion – how was Captain Christie going to squeeze Wagner into a miniature opera house? For that is what it still was. Discarding the first idea of 150 seats, the Theatre Where Things Would Be Done Properly had 300, which was still miniature, for Wagner. A rich man's whim, to advance his young wife's career. So it was said.

Evening dress was recommended, though the owner-founder was frequently to be seen in an ensemble of white tie, tails and battered plimsolls.

How many other opera houses in the world had a landing ground for aeroplanes – this was in 1934 – just a hundred yards from the building? That was for the ultra-chic. Those without car or chauffeur, or with no liking for a long drive, had been catered for. A special train would depart, mid-afternoon, from Victoria Station.

During the interval, dinner would be served in the restaurant, prior notice being requested. The cuisine was superb, a fact taken for granted by those who recalled Captain Christie's letter to his mother from the trenches, asking her to engage a chef from the Café Royal for his leave, as her cook was not worth training. Also, a rare alternative was offered. Those with their own transport and enough room might care to bring hampers . . . they were welcome to use the restaurant . . . it might be more convenient to bring their own butler.

The last couple of months before the opening were so busy that one plan was shelved: it had been hoped to install kennels and provide meals for visitors' dogs.

Curiouser and curiouser – the ladies in the cast found that their lavatories had doors wide enough to allow crinolines to pass through; how obvious, but who else would have thought of it?

The lady of the house now had a toddler daughter in the nursery; she was hostess to a full house party, and she was singing Susanna in the opening *Figaro*. She was also in the early stages of another pregnancy. Few prima donnas could have taken that workload calmly, but Audrey did, and on the last day of that year she gave birth to George.

Seasons came and went; audiences crowded, and audiences sparse; losses from £7,000 to £10,000 and then right down to £4,000, due less to the opera than to John's knowledge of wines; his cellar did a roaring trade, and extensions were built. The theatre was extended too, making room for another hundred people; all done by Ringmer Building Works. It was frenetic, and Audrey succumbed. She had often suffered from throat trouble, and now it was worse than ever. She convalesced abroad and alone, pondering that she and John had a most beautiful home but no time to enjoy it; a home for the benefit of everyone but themselves. And she had to come abroad for a holiday.

'Some day, John darling, let's have a holiday there!'

The peacetime thirties were full of unemployment, and the *Magic Flute* of 1937 had an unusual chorus. The men were all Welsh. Normally their working hours were spent in the mines or the tinworks, or the great boiler factories. There, they could find no work, but here – God bless John Christie – he was paying them to sing!

Rosamund and George, the small Christies, took it mostly in their stride, though there was the odd misconception. Taken to a neighbour's party, George seemed for a while preoccupied. Then he went to his hostess.

'Where do you keep your opera house?'

His mother was feeling better and made arrangements for twenty-five children from the London slums to spend a fortnight at Glyndebourne. Her own holiday would come some day.

John's first impulse when war was declared was to evacuate Audrey and the children to Canada. Government financial restrictions left her with little money, and it was hard to manage. She was able to earn by giving occasional concerts; John used his clothing ration to send warm things for her and the children. He regretted having parted from them, for without Audrey he felt lost. One good thing came of it: she met Sir Thomas Beecham, whose attitude to Glyndebourne hitherto had been 'I do not wish to know.' John had written many times, asking him to appear at Glyndebourne, and all the letters had been ignored. Yet, meeting Audrey alone, he was impressed. John received a telegram: 'Have just conducted two performances of Mozart's *Figaro* in which Audrey as Susanna has scored a brilliant and special success... Beecham.'

All this, and Heaven too; perhaps not quite Heaven, but Audrey and the children were invited to use the Beecham flat in New York. It was a great boost to the budget, until in the spring of 1944 they were able to return home.

Peace came to Europe but not to Glyndebourne. Beecham, still basking in the memory of Audrey's performance, offered to conduct when the opera house re-opened in 1945. He would conduct without a fee – on his terms, naturally. The offer was accepted – on John Christie's terms.

Beecham wanted the best 'without regard for subsidiary considerations' – i.e. political or financial. Not that Christie was much given to consideration of financial matters, but he wanted British talent ('Non-existent,' said Beecham), young talent ('Since when have I been a kindergarten nurse?' asked Sir Thomas), and the Glyndebourne battle was rounded off by the

Employment, elegance and enchantment – Glyndebourne

two wives exchanging letters in which their husbands' views were expressed with biting yet courteous clarity. Betty wrote 'with affection' and Audrey replied 'ever affectionately', after which the proposed collaboration ceased even to be a proposal.

That was the year of Britten's first opera, *Peter Grimes*. Its successor, *The Rape of Lucretia*, was ready. There were fourteen performances at Glyndebourne in 1946, with Kathleen Ferrier as Lucretia; in 1947 came *Albert Herring*. The quarrel with Beecham had been patched up; he lived on the estate for a time, and conducted for John, though not in opera.

Then came the Festival of Britain; even Christie was feeling his financial losses but the Government offered a grant towards the production of four Mozart operas, and the John Lewis Partnership offered more. All was well – except that damaged eye. It was hurting, probably spreading infection . . . he had it out.

Audrey would not be in the Festival performances, having been sent to hospital, but she helped John to work out the foundation of the Glyndebourne Trust. Within the year, she was dead.

There were sparse compensations. His sight had not gone completely. In due course he could see George's pretty bride, and later he was almost inseparable from his grandson Hector. *Fidelio* was a success. He had said so all along, but no one would believe him. That, and Hector, made up for a lot. But not for Audrey.

One evening during the 1962 season, the family and close friends gathered round his bed. Downstairs, opera-goers were gathering for *Cosí fan Tutte*. Glyndebourne would continue, just as he and Audrey had planned.

Christie had inescapable memories of the trenches in the Great War. From those came his efforts to help those men who arrived home to unemployment.

Few had similar wealth, though their memories were similar. A tiny gratuity was probably the greatest sum many had ever possessed; many ached for peace and quiet, and they could seek it on only the very smallest scale – not in a big ugly house such as Christie had inherited, but something very small and as cheap as possible. If only it could be in a beautiful place.

In 1916 an advertisement appeared in the national press, like a promise of Paradise. A wealthy developer, Charles Neville, had purchased 600 acres of land east of Rottingdean, to build an estate of small homes. Plots nearest the sea were priced at £100; those just behind, at £75; those further inland were only £50. Most interesting of all, there would be a competition. Whoever suggested the best name for the estate would be awarded one of the best plots, and there would be fifty consolation prizes of one £50 plot each.

Mr Kemp of Maidstone and Mr West of Ilford shared that first prize, both having suggested 'New Anzac on Sea'. Almost immediately came the tragedy of Gallipoli, so 'Peacehaven' was substituted. That was the idea of over 200 people, who found that in taking up their prizes they were expected to pay 3 guineas in legal fees – as much as two weeks' wages for some; those, at least, who were lucky enough to be earning wages at all. Some intrepid folk took Mr Neville to court and were awarded refunds. Others, numbed by wartime suffering, were apathetic; it was just another disappointement. Many never came to see their prizes. Great spaces between the few houses were taken over by the Agricultural Board to grow food.

By 1920 the area was again marked out into plots, again on the grid system. Streets were named after Sussex towns and beauty spots; some, after people involved in the project. Searle Avenue was named after the very first owner to build there.

Once again building began, in a somewhat do-it-yourself fashion, for materials were scarce, but Government backing for 'homes for heroes' was some help. Peacehaven heroes also had their own song and their own newspaper, the *Peacehaven Post*, run by Charles Neville.

He was no cigar-flourishing tycoon; in the early days he had lived on the site in an asbestos hut while the surveyors were at work, and his smart car was not always in evidence. There were similarities to Glyndebourne: Peacehaven had its own brick and concrete block factory, and its own sawmill and joinery works. By 1922 over a thousand men were employed there.

Neville was publicity-minded. Much information was given out, complete with artists' impressions, as to what Peacehaven would eventually look like: the trees, the gardens, the shops, the schools, the electric railway. Notwithstanding the trouble over that first competition, he organized another to encourage more people to buy plots, the winner to receive a free, ready-built house. This time all went smoothly, and there was a repeat performance some years later.

Even so, there were still too many vacancies, though all the Churches were represented by temporary buildings, and several private schools were functioning. Community spirit was strong, and a few celebrities were attracted. Felix Powell, who wrote 'Pack up Your Troubles' – John Christie might have been more familiar with that than Charles Neville, but Powell lived at Peacehaven. The novelist Graham Greene took one look and declared that it was like a frontier town, with its roads cut at right angles in an unyielding geometrical system. But that supreme artist among folk singers, Bob Copper, has lived there for many years. The community has also produced a Miss Great Britain.

As in Crawley New Town, everything hinges upon the same fact: tastes differ. Some like it, others do not. In Peacehaven, the latter persuasion were so numerous by the outbreak of the 1939 war that once again the government, this time in the guise of the Ministry of Agriculture, stepped in and used the empty plots as agricultural land. Afterwards, Peacehaven went on as before, providing a few more homes, a lot of open space and the same old controversy.

'... this bungaloid excrescence ...'

'... the greatest flowering of bungalow architecture in England ...'

Those who chose to live there used hard-earned money to do so. Their decision and their admirable effort deserve respect.

Sussex villages provide an inexhaustible subject; their origins, names, history, architecture and people – all are full of interest. There are two with an even greater claim to fame, because they were created specially for children.

Both belong to East Sussex: one is at Chailey, north of Lewes, where Chailey Common is a 400-acre nature reserve; the other is in the historic village of Sedlescombe. The Heritage Craft School at Chailey takes children of all ages; the Pestalozzi Village at Sedlescombe takes them from the age of ten, for as long as ten years. Though both villages aim to give their children every available opportunity, their starting points differ.

Pestalozzi has earlier roots. When Napoleon devastated Europe, there were many child victims. Pestalozzi, a Swiss, suggested that all European countries might work together to make reparation. After the 1939 war his idea really burgeoned in the hands of another Swiss, Walter Corti. He set up a children's village for war orphans, no matter what nationality; the world sat up and took notice, and progress was swift.

Each village was a group of homes, each one for children of one particular nationality, cared for by a compatriot house-mother, rather than being decanted into an assortment of languages and customs. They felt safe within familiar surroundings; not so much in the fabric of the home but the companionship provided. At the same time there were frequent contacts with Pestalozzi homes of other nationalities, creating a sense of community as a whole.

The English village was founded in 1958, when Oatlands Park estate at Sedlescombe was for sale; Sir Hugh Casson designed the first house. Almost immediately there came a change of emphasis, after the closure of the last refugee camps in Europe. Pestalozzi were no longer seeking only war orphans, but the victims of poverty, particularly in the Third World; those whose intelligence warranted a better education than they could receive at home. Given a wide practical as well as academic education, in the company of as many nationalities as Pestalozzi could provide, they would eventually be more beneficial to their own countries than a score of imposed bureaucrats. They are constantly in touch with their families and return home regularly for holidays at the expense of the foundation, however far it may be. At present the Sussex village has about ninety children, but this will shortly increase thanks to an enormous donation making it possible to build and endow another house. Good causes, even of international status, rarely receive donations of such proportions, but the potential of the Pestalozzi villages for world peace make one hope that there will be many more.

Chailey Heritage is differently placed, having been adopted by the Ministry of Health nearly forty years ago. The idea was born a century after that of Pestalozzi, but it was put into action immediately, catering for crippled children of all ages. In its early days at the turn of the century, handicaps were often the result of malnutrition, and diseases such as rickets or the ubiquitous tuberculosis; now they are often the result of thalidomide and road accidents. Chailey is unlikely to become redundant.

Crippled children once faced a hopeless future. They, and disabled adults, had long been the concern of Dr Kimmins, Chief Inspector of LCC schools at the end of the last century. His wife shared his concern, and feeling for the loneliness of such people, had organized a Guild, holding regular afternoon meetings in Southwark. It gave them companionship, and ensured that they were informed about the help and advice which were even then available. Isolation had been a great burden.

The Guild was also a source of information to Mrs Kimmins, and there was little to cheer her. Some of the children needed residential care; all needed training to be able to earn a living in spite of handicaps – pride must be rehabilitated. She worked out the pros and closed her eyes to the cons; Chailey's beginnings were simple. Seven disabled boys; £5 in cash; and one derelict, rat-infested workhouse at Chailey.

From then on, the history of that place has been a study in miracles. The whole purpose was to treat, to teach and to train. Education must suit individual capacity; medical treatment must be the best obtainable; training must impart skills to give the children a future of independence and fulfilment.

The personality of Mrs Kimmins attracted many benefactors; she had an irresistible glow. The derelict workhouse was gradually replaced by beautiful buildings, and in 1908 a Heritage was founded for girls, also at Chailey. Many crafts were taught by experts who gave their time; woodwork, silversmithing, shoemaking, dressmaking, weaving – whatever a child's aptitude, instruction would be obtained.

Can one call it a curiosity – this home of miracles, the outcome of one woman's determination, filled with joy which is immediately sensed by visitors?

There are curiosities in the girls' chapel: carved oak panels and altar furniture; normal things to find in any chapel, except that these were made by someone who shared the children's enthusiasm for handicrafts: a royal Duchess. She was the very first Patroness of Chailey, herself a talented woodcarver and silversmith – Princess Louise, Duchess of Argyll. Imagine a child full of admiration for such work, sitting up in the bed where lessons must be done; silversmithing on a miniature forge with specially designed shields (made of course in the carpentry shop); that child's heritage, the precious opportunity to achieve the apparently impossible.

Curious, yes. Miracles always are.

5 Paradoxically

This is the tale of a tiny church. When William of Normandy landed at Pevensey, St Paul's Church had already served Elsted for three score years and two; given the Normans' propensity for making use of buildings already in existence, it was predictable that they would extend rather than rebuild.

Elsted church had been built in the times of Edward the Confessor; it was just the right size for the needs of a small hamlet on the slopes of the north-western Downs. It was thirty feet long and half as wide, and every little stone was placed with loving care; the walls are as perfect an example of Saxon herringbone masonry as one could wish to see.

Towards the end of the twelfth century more space was needed; Norman builders cut through the eastern wall, making a smooth rounded archway as it is today, and extending the building into a small chancel. In the north wall, two more archways led to a new aisle; obviously the congregation had considerably increased. At the same time, a new style was gradually evolving; the Early English. When the Norman chancel had to be replaced by a larger one, it was in that style, with dainty lancet windows.

Those were the opening chapters of the story; the only addition for some time was a porch, built in the seventeenth century. The real excitement came towards the mid-nineteenth century when St Paul's Church was showing signs of age. Extensive repairs were essential, and the estimated cost was more than the villagers could possibly meet. The incumbent approached the wealthy lady who was patroness of the parish; the living was in her gift. He had high hopes – St Paul's would soon be put to rights.

The Hon. Mrs Vincent Harcourt had other ideas. Rather than patch up so dilapidated a building, she would build a new one, on a different site – higher up, so that the spire would be visible for many miles around. It was a mile further for Elsted villagers to walk; 'If they want to worship, they will come'. So she said.

Elsted church, beloved for a thousand years

She meant well; indeed, she was being eminently reasonable, from her own point of view. Old Treyford church, a little younger than Elsted, was in a similarly parlous state; it was higher on the Downs, next to an ancient manor house, serving only a tiny community. The rector was also asking help to repair that. To an essentially practical person, it was logical to build one new church half-way between the two ancient buildings. Bearing in mind her particular lifestyle, one sees that she had no idea of the difference between a mile travelled in a barouche, or even a governess cart, and an uphill mile travelled on foot. Therefore a splendid new church, St Peter's, was built half-way between Elsted and Treyford.

Parishioners certainly wanted to worship, but St Paul's was their church. Some even stayed away; it was an almost unthinkable thing in those days, but the ruins might be unsafe, and St Peter's seemed unhomelike, so they stayed away. Nearly twenty years passed, and a partial, tentative restoration of St Paul's took place. That Norman aisle which had once been a valuable enlargement, though it made the building colder in winter, was removed. Those who wished might return to their old place of worship. The new church up at Treyford had, in common with a few others in similar positions, received the title 'Cathedral of the Downs', but its use was more dutiful than affectionate.

In 1893 St Paul's congregation numbered about twenty – just right for so small a building; but a violent storm crashed a tree across the roof, demolishing that carefully restored nave. Only the chancel was left, with the Norman arch open to the sky. That was soon closed with corrugated iron, and the company of the faithful crowded into a space which amounted to about a quarter of the original church. They continued like that until after the Second World War.

St Paul's had seen hard times; what of the new church? There were worrying signs; after a survey, the spire and nave were condemned as unsafe. Even so, it was hoped that the chancel might be saved – which may have sounded familiar to the people of Elsted.

Partial demolition of St Peter's proved useless; the whole edifice was dangerous, and it was demolished with explosives. The parish was short of a chancel.

The ancient church at Treyford was past help, and the incumbent, the Reverend Fernley J. Parkhouse, concentrated upon his appeal for funds to repair St Paul's. It was one of the most enterprising parochial appeals ever launched, and the response was generous. Expatriates in the USA, adults and children nationwide, the national Press – money which had come only sparsely for Treyford St Peter's came eagerly for St Paul's. Best of all, HM Queen Elizabeth the Queen Mother (then the Queen) gave a set of silver teaspoons and sugar tongs to be raffled. In 1951, on the last day of November, St Paul's Church, carefully restored, was re-dedicated.

Go inside. It is light, loved, brisk, as lively a church as one could imagine, even when empty. It is small, simple and superb;

The Cathedral of the Downs

nearly a thousand years old, and likely to be loved for as long again.

Travel up the hill to the place where tall trees surround the site of St Peter's Church. Nothing remains but traces of the aisle and some graves.

Yet there is something else. Those four walls, made of tall, sombre trees instead of stone, stand protectively around the place where once a spire soared proudly, visible for miles around. Now there is no spire, no pride. But within those high trees there is quietude, as if, in its demise, that Cathedral of the Downs has acquired the grace and peace which were absent before. The smaller, older church has won the race; yet in losing, the high, proud church has gained something wonderful, intangible. In dying, it came to life.

Elsted church is a mere adolescent when compared to Bosham. The walls of that church contain materials used by the Romans in their basilica, formerly on this site. Holy Trinity has been in existence so long (though not always under that name) that it is a Vicar of Bray among churches. Used by successive invaders and settlers, with each latest arrival warring against those who followed (or vice versa), this small building contains mementoes of more diverse peoples, periods and persuasions than Pevensey.

There was a small, early religious community in Bosham headed by an Irishman, Dicul. He had no influence upon the surrounding Saxons, unless one accepts as negative evidence the lack of any tradition that he met a violent end at their hands. They resembled the little girl in the nursery rhyme: when they were good, they were very very good, but when otherwise they were violently anti-Christian. Dicul and his monks would seem to have been fortunate.

Sometime between the eighth and tenth centuries the Saxons had a change of heart and began to build the church. Roman materials were on the site; indeed, part of the Roman foundations were still useful; they were of excellent quality, and time-saving, though when the Saxons had finished they had built a nave, a chancel and a tower entirely in their own style. It was of course a dual-purpose building: within such stout walls, women, children and the elderly could be gathered as in a fortress during an attack; the windows in the north clerestory were built so high that it would have been almost impossible to aim missiles at those sheltering inside.

The tower needed two look-out slits facing outwards across the creek, for the next invaders were on their way. Those fearsome longboats, each one propelled strongly and smoothly by the human force within, could be seen in time for word to pass round that the Danes were approaching. Saxon to Dane, Dane to Saxon – both sides were vicious. Captured Danes were flayed alive; Bosham church door, entry to the sanctuary of the religion of gentle forgiveness, might well be adorned with strips of Danish skin, hastily nailed up after yet another execution.

Eventually the Danes gained more than a foothold. Canute was a wise king with less brutality to his credit than most. A tradition through the centuries said that his eight-year-old daughter died here and was buried in the church. Tradition even knew the location of her grave, but few believed it.

In 1865 the incumbent wanted to know. He asked permission and excavated. Tradition had been right. A small stone coffin, in the right place and of the right period, held the remains of a little child. The daughter of a Danish king had been carried to her grave through the door where conquered Danes' skin had been displayed.

The font is another paradoxical object. A receptacle for holy water, for the sacrament of baptism as approved by Christ: it still has the staples necessary to lock a lid into position when not in use. Holy water was an essential ingredient in many superstitious rites and magic spells; too many people – hell-bent, as it were – helped themselves.

The chapel in the south aisle is much higher than the rest of the church, for there is a crypt beneath. Crypts are usually basement constructions. In Bosham church it actually rises five feet above the nave floor. Fortunately part of it also lies beneath in the orthodox manner; an entirely upstairs crypt would be even more curious.

The chancel has several corbels, of which the most vivid is that of a monk putting his tongue out; one would like to think that some later stonemason was quietly giving Dicul his revenge. Perchance artisans may not have heard of that patient monk; yet if tradition held so strongly to its knowledge of Canute's daughter, the possibility is strong.

The little daughter of Canute was probably buried in Bosham

If Bosham church was dual purpose, its door was multi-purpose. Used as an exhibition stand for the remnants of beaten foes, in later years, when Crusaders returned from the Holy Land – having killed numerous Saracens – they blunted their sword tips on the stonework of the first church they entered after landing. Bosham was well placed for such attentions, and the crusaders' crosses, holy graffiti, are still there on the stone porch; reputedly a sign that a sword used in defence of the Holy Land must never be used in lesser causes. No doubt they all had a few spares.

Explain it if you can. The Peacehaven site was chosen, the roads were marked neatly, the plots classified and priced; everyone concerned did their best. And after over sixty years it still attracts harsh criticism and even abuse.

The Winchelsea site was chosen, the roads marked neatly, the plots classified and priced; everyone concerned did their best. It was recently described as 'altogether enchanting'.

Unfair? Perhaps the slight difference in time has a bearing on the matter; I ought to have mentioned it . . . after over 700 years, it was recently described as 'altogether enchanting'.

It happened when the old town of Winchelsea, then lying at sea level, was constantly battered by Channel storms, and its destruction seemed imminent. The King (Edward I) decided to move the town. It was one of the Cinque Ports, so the Warden of the Cinque Ports of that time, Stephen de Penchester, was told to proceed, using a site to the north where the ground was higher.

This site was smaller than Peacehaven, only 150 acres compared to 600. The streets were marked out in a grid pattern; the overall shape was triangular rather than rectangular, but the houses were similarly arranged in rectangular blocks.

The disposal of plots was more complicated than at Peacehaven, with its three simple types. At Winchelsea there were 79 harbour plots, 610 town plots, 23 plots outside the western walls, and 90 suburban plots to the south, which must have been very cheap. It involved some tricky mathematics; the total rents from all 802 plots must add up exactly to the rent the King would have received from all the property he had set aside for the new town. He demanded no extra; he expected no less; Stephen de Penchester must be precise. At the same time all plots must be fairly valued. A poor man hacking away at a suburban plot which could be ruined in minutes by the sea or the French, must pay far less than the merchant building his fine house within the walls. It was a far cry from Peacehaven's front, middle and back rows.

Though the latter had its origins during the Great War, the buildings planned had no provision against possible future hostilities. Winchelsea was among those towns on the south-east coast which had suffered terribly not only from the elements but from many fierce raids by the French. The new town was provided with stoutly constructed cellars; wisely so, for the French had by no means finished, though the sea had done its worst. The Sussex map by Speede (1610) shows an offshore patch like a sandbank, marked 'Old Winchelsea Drowned'.

New Winchelsea was not drowned; rather the reverse, for it was planned as a port, being on the estuary of the Brede, which at that time widened into a useful harbour; unfortunately, the sea turned contrary and receded; within two centuries the new port had ceased to function.

While the sea receded, the French advanced again and again; though Winchelsea was built with walls, as well as cellars for

A fine example of new town planning: Winchelsea, commenced in 1283

underground shelters, still the attackers stormed in, devastating everything. To this day one can feel the measure of terror and despair which was rife in the town. One of the gates – New Gate – which was intended to be one of the entrances, stands solitary, way out towards Hastings, for all the world as though it has no connection with the town along the road. Half of St Thomas' Church still stands; no one knows whether it was once complete, and then half demolished by raiders; or whether it was half-built, and the builders gave it up as a lost cause.

So much horror, followed by centuries of stillness; a town in a state of shock, yet exactly as it was described: enchanting. For its counterpart, so similar in conception and planning, 'enchanting' is hardly the right word, even to Peacehaven's most partisan resident. One might as well compare a Gainsborough duchess with a 1920s flapper.

Perhaps that is the heart of the matter. Peacehaven needs only another 700 years.

Not only the sea can be wayward; human beings have just a trace of that characteristic. Winchelsea is enchanting after 700 years; Peacehaven is unenchanting after a mere sixty; similarly the railways. Steam-engines were officially taken out of service, and diesels were substituted. Therefore steam, being obsolete, is romantic; diesel, used every day, is dull. It is the old fantasy of Respect for the Dead; the hushed *Nil Nisi Bonum* over the deceased's sherry, whereas only a week previously no holds were barred. It used to be unwise to take a corner seat in steam days, for the carriage window had to be opened and shut with pesty regularity; a bend in the track or a gust of wind, and the compartment would be filled with choking smoke and smuts. The corner passenger was nearest. I sat on Grandmother's lap while she tut-tutted over a great smut, lodged in my eye. 'Surely someone could invent cleaner trains than this!'

They did. Years later, I sat in a lovingly restored Bluebell train, while another smut lodged itself in the eye of an old gentleman. He was in considerable discomfort as he endeavoured to extract it. With a beatific smile, he remarked to his fellow passengers – 'Steam has such *personality*!'

It must be admitted that more than waywardness is involved. Is it appreciation of industrial history or admiration for a wonderful invention?

Whatever the reason, steam trains and their smuts are now curiosities, and greatly cherished. There are numerous small lines, privately owned, run by volunteer enthusiasts, and the very first was the Bluebell Line in 1960.

Railways in the late 1950s frequently fell victim to the Beeching axe, and steam-engines, even historic examples, were sent to the scrapyards. It was more than enthusiasts could bear: replacement by diesel was bad enough, but destruction was beyond endurance. They took action; funds were raised – not

Next spring, travel by steam train through bluebell-carpeted countryside

enough to purchase, but they were able to lease five miles of redundant track from British Rail, and in little more than a year the Bluebell Railway became the first fun line. It ran between Sheffield Park and Horsted Keynes, and in the first season alone it attracted more passengers than the enthusiasts had ever thought possible: 50,000, a figure which has steadily increased through the years.

Not the least curious point of the whole enterprise is the wide cross-section of people who join together in this common interest, one so absorbing that most of their free time is given without question. One attraction must be that it is possible to rise from the ranks. Volunteer status confers no privileges; would-be engine-drivers do not turn up on a Sunday morning, climb into the nearest cab and try their hand. An engine-cleaner learns something about engines; if he perseveres, he learns more as he goes on. Having proved possession of that quality – perseverance – he may, if there is a vacancy, become a fireman. If he has the patience to wait for that rarest of vacancies – for an engine-driver – he will start with shunting duties. It all takes time and is only for the enthusiast.

There is a story of a stationmaster who retired early to devote more time to the Bluebell Line. He wanted to learn to be an engine-driver; steam-engines, you understand. He did, too. It must have been the classic case of patience and perseverance.

Presumably the volunteer drivers and firemen get hot and thirsty after a day's work on the Bluebell Line, though I never discovered whether authenticity is carried to the extent of quaffing bottles of cold tea.

There were hot and thirsty workers in Heathfield when the parish church had been seriously damaged by fire. Rebuilding was going to be a long job. It all had to be done by hand in 1380, and many workmen were needed. So a public house/inn/tavern/hostelry was built specially for them. They called it 'The Star'.

You can still get a drink there, though it might not be the same brand.

If you go to Amberley, rejoice and be exceeding glad, for it is of surpassing loveliness. Go for a treasure hunt, your quarry being one of the few cottages in that village which has a tiled roof instead of thatch. It will be easy to find; the name is on the gate: The Thatched Cottage.

Go down to Amberley Wild Brooks, but if you are clutching an Ordnance Survey map and ask residents the way to South Path, luck will not be on your side. They know it as Peat Path, with good reason, for it was long a peat-cutting area. Now, it is flat, peaceful – sluggish, even; the brooks seem stagnant rather than wild, but 'wild' in this case does not mean riproaring – merely a corruption of Wealden, which makes better sense. Actually the brooks which have been tamed – that is to say, controlled by sluice gates – are far more lively than the wild ones.

The best time of year to visit Amberley Wild Brooks is November. Wear wellingtons because the mudflat known as Peat Path resembles wet cement; palest grey, deep and sticky, making even one's own footsteps inaudible. There will be no one else in sight; birds are hushed, cows are distant, and the gentle trickle of the tamed brooks is the length of Peat Path away. The silence is a benediction and grace.

Go back past the church, around the side of the castle, and learn a most valuable lesson if you do not know it already.

Amberley Wild Brooks, tamed by a sluice

Dreams are at their best when still unrealized. There is an old tag about an Englishman's home being his castle. Fine; but supposing a castle becomes his home? More than a few visitors pass Amberley, Arundel, Bodiam and the rest with a passing twinge of wishful thinking.

In the early days, defence of castles was not only possible, it was expected, taken for granted. Look up at Amberley's great curtain wall; intruders could be driven away by arrows, or in later years by gunfire; from the top of the wall they could be sent packing with boiling oil, molten lead, stones or whatever else came to hand.

In these civilized days, many visitors assume that anything crenellated is public property, and they walk in. Portcullises cannot seal every gateway; the cost would be prohibitive. The rich man in his castle has not been rich for many a long year, for repairs are expensive and frequently necessary. Moving out is no option, for though a castle strains the purse-strings, it is as deeply loved as the tiniest and prettiest of Amberley's thatched cottages. The cottager can fix a gate with a bolt; the castellan's only defence is the written word – KEEP OUT – which is ineffective against the obtuse. Life in a castle is less than ideal for those who are not gregarious.

Good news is everywhere if only you look hard enough, and this is special.
    Chichester is a reformed city. It is sedate and beautiful, with everything to entrance the historian, the architect, the tourist, the gourmet; even the sailing enthusiast has everything he needs within a few minutes' drive. Everyone is content, and never a cross word is uttered. It was not so in the days of the first Elizabeth.
    Her Majesty came to visit a friend; sitting in his elegant house, she heard the unmistakeable noise of rioting from the end of the street. She sighed.
    'Quite a little London.'
    Which is why, when you visit the white museum at the end of that peaceful row of shops and houses, you are walking in Little London. The name remained, though the tumult and the shouting died long since. Chichester is a reformed city.

The Blue Idol: it could be something from a curio shop; an exhibit in a museum; a public house; something extracted from a shipwreck, or part of buried treasure. An evocative name, but hardly to be associated with a dwelling-house. Which is what the Blue Idol is.
    It is a picturesque, long, timber-framed house at Coolham. The timbers are close-set, for they support a roof of Horsham Slabs, and there is no heavier roof than that. It is still sturdy after 400 years; the builders knew what they were doing.
    The builders did not know that fanciful name; in its earlier days the house was known as Little Slatters. When in later times the Society of Friends, the Quakers, were persecuted, Little Slatters was owned by a Quaker, John Shaw, who allowed Meeting to be held in his house. William Penn, afterwards the founder of Pennsylvania, was one of the worshippers here. The Society was so numerous that John Shaw had one end of his house converted into a proper meeting-room; a lofty one, for he had the first floor removed, leaving a light, airy room.

That room is still used for Meeting, and the rest of the house is a guesthouse for Quakers or any others who need peace and rest. But some time between the days of John Shaw and the last century, it lost that pretty name, Little Slatters, and became the Blue Idol. No one knows why. The change probably occurred during the seventy years prior to 1869. During that time it was not used as a meeting-house, and it is said that the owner painted the walls blue.

One has to concentrate to the point of desperation to imagine that beautiful old house turning blue between its timbers. Surely only one kind of householder would perpetrate such a misdemeanour: one with more money than taste; one intent upon drawing attention to himself and his dwelling; one who worshipped possessions above all else.

Cringing at the sight, a Quaker, recalling quietly the days gone by, might murmur to himself – 'A Blue Idol . . .'

The Cokelers of Loxwood dressed to suit the nineteenth century, but their business acumen would have done credit to the most go-getting twentieth-century New Yorker. They felt that they, and they alone, knew the way to Heaven; yet if any stranger ventured to join their services, they welcomed him delightedly. Their founder, John Sirgood, was a married man, but the Cokelers as a sect disapproved of marriage, for devotion to a partner obscured one's view of God.

John Sirgood, a London shoemaker, preached regularly on Clapham Common; then he saw in a dream that there were villagers in Sussex who would not only listen but follow his teaching. He and his wife had little travelling money, so they went by wheelbarrow; one rode, one pushed, turn and turn about all the way to Sussex. They did not settle in Loxwood, but he preached regularly there and gained a large following. Their proper name was 'The Dependents', and it is still to be seen on their neat chapel. They were dependent upon the Lord and one another. The name by which they have generally been known is 'The Cokelers' – only a nickname, gained from their habit of serving cocoa between their religious services, but it stuck.

Those religious services were a problem. There were three on Sundays and two more during the week, but Cokelers were working people whose free time was rare. The many domestic

At Loxwood: the chapel of the gentle Cokelers

servants who joined the sect normally had only one day off, once a month. Sirgood and the Elders discussed the problem and produced the great idea: a store. They already had some communal savings, intended for a better chapel in the distant future, but this was a more pressing need. They built and stocked a little store. Personal savings were also invested; work was provided for many of the members – an ever-increasing number, for many non-Cokeler residents patronized the venture, which was well run and increasingly well stocked. Nothing was too much trouble for the antique-looking shopkeepers. Small wonder.

Their rule of life forbade listening to secular music, reading books other than the Bible, bringing flowers into the house, and of course drinking and smoking. Bearing in mind the time they saved through remaining unmarried and therefore having no demanding home ties, it is understandable that the store was their main interest other than chapel. Their waking hours, their savings – all were devoted to that one purpose; it soon employed all Cokelers who needed to work there. With so much effort and interest, trade flourished. Cokeler communities in other districts also ran stores, and before long members travelling from one community to another, usually to preach, were able to have bed and breakfast at the stores, which also came to the rescue if any Cokeler fell upon hard times.

They were in this world, but not of it; they disapproved of the ways of the rest of humanity, sure that God felt the same; they were the Chosen – yet they welcomed strangers with loving generosity.

Dressed in the prim mode of a past century and following a very restricted life, they felt so strongly that matrimony shut out God that they preferred to allow a trial marriage for two years in the hope that the couple concerned would change their minds before being finally committed.

From the thousands of the 1930s they have dwindled to just a tiny group. The stores closed long ago; the chapel, though as neat as ever, is used only for funerals. Cokelers are hardly ever to be seen. They were the Chosen Ones, and if they all felt and spoke with the spontaneous warmth which I, a stranger, heard on the telephone, they were indeed well chosen. We shall be the poorer for their passing, and it is to be hoped that their memory will be kept alive in some way. Perhaps that little chapel will be allowed to remain, tucked modestly away in a corner of Loxwood village.

6 Architecturally

Architecturally, Sussex has a little charmer; a winner from any viewpoint, with the added distinction of being the first building ever purchased by the National Trust.

Low, decoratively timbered, and thatched; so pretty that one could stand enthralled, oblivious to all else; this chocolate-box confection was built long before chocolate boxes were invented, about half-way through the fourteenth century, when the nearby church was constructed. It was a home for the priest: Clergy House, Alfriston. The church was the largest for miles around; one of those accorded the title of 'Cathedral of the Downs'.

Through the centuries Clergy House gave the priests a home; perhaps the Reformation temporarily took it out of their hands, but it returned. By the nineteenth century it was in very poor condition. No longer occupied by priests, it had long been useful in housing farm labourers and their families. The vicar was still responsible for its upkeep, and complained that he could not afford the expense. In 1885 the Ecclesiastical Commissioners assented to its demolition.

This was not so simple. One old woman was still in occupation, the last member of labouring families who had lived there for over a century. Her plea to be left in peace in her declining days was irresistible and she was left undisturbed. In 1888 she died, but by that time the vicar was ready to retire.

His successor was a conservationist who loved Clergy House at first sight. The Reverend Mr Beynon turned to the Sussex Archaeological Society for advice; they agreed that it must at all costs be preserved, but one-man fund-raising was slow work. He persevered for five years, then events took a magical turn for the better. In 1894 the National Trust was born. Beynon was introduced to one of the three founders, Canon Rawnsley. As soon as the Trust was a going concern, Clergy House was purchased from the Ecclesiastical Commissioners. £10 changed hands.

This may sound like a knock-down price, but at that juncture

Clergy House, the first building purchased by the National Trust

it was a knock-down house. To restore it, two years' work and £855 were needed. It must be remembered that money values differed greatly from ours. That old woman last living in Clergy House had never in her life seen as much as £1 weekly wage – perhaps 10 shillings, with a few extras in kind; to her, £855 would have been wealth untold.

It was wisely used. The easy and far cheaper way would have been to repair the house with any suitable material available. The National Trust restored it with historical accuracy. Wattle and daub did not receive a nice new coat of whitewash. Medieval builders used lime and tallow to render those walls waterproof, and that is how they were treated. The floor could have been simply boarded over; medieval style, it was rammed – not with clay but with lumps of chalk rammed until they were smooth and shiny, as in the making of a dew pond. But the pond would be prevented from drying out by the water in it, and the rain and mist which fell upon it; the floor in a house might well dry out quickly in the warmth. Medieval builders avoided that by mixing the chalk with sour milk; the very slight grease content acted as a seal. Clergy House was a clear indication of the quality of the Trust's future work.

Alfriston was a busy place in medieval times. The little Clergy House nestled near the Cathedral of the Downs, housing the priest; the Star Inn, sturdily timbered beneath its roof of Horsham slabs, was lavishly ornamented with carvings of religious import, as befitted a hostelry which specialized in accommodating pilgrims. Three shrines lay within travelling distance; St Richard, St Thomas and St Swithin, at Chichester, Canterbury and Winchester respectively. A number of such inns sprang up in medieval times, and they were kept very busy. A pilgrimage was the package tour of the period; Chaucer blamed springtime for the urge to be up and doing:

> Whan that Aprille with his shoures sote
> The droghte of Marche hath perced to the rote . . .
>
> Than longen folk to goon on pilgrimages.

They travelled in groups, met different people, saw unfamiliar places and at the same time fulfilled spiritual obligations. Inns like the Star were built for the comfort of pilgrims many of whom were not short of the odd groat; there had been another inn on the same site before the Star reared its splendid head. Perhaps they had received something like the present-day assurance that any inconvenience during alterations was regretted, for those alterations were the most expensive available. The roof was magnificent. No leaking or blazing thatch would disturb pilgrims there; Horsham slabs were used. Each one weighed about half a hundredweight (about 25 kilograms). They were cut from a laminated sandstone mined at Horsham or Slinfold, but the weight, and the difficulty of working such tough material, made it very expensive indeed. So much so that, whenever a house with such a roof was demolished, the Horsham slabs would be bought secondhand and taken elsewhere for re-use. Therefore the roof tiles we see today on houses such as the Blue Idol and the Star may well be at least twice as old as the buildings beneath, having roofed some other building during its lifetime in ancient days. There is an account surviving from 1357: 'In purchase of one house at Horsham with stone, 66sh and 9d; in expenses of divers men carrying the said stones to Westmeston, 3sh and 6d.'

Churches and barns were also roofed with Horsham slabs; massive timbers were necessary to support such weight. You have only to go inside the Blue Idol or the Star to understand this. Such timbers were expensive; they must be carefully selected, expertly felled, patiently seasoned and cut only by the most experienced craftsmen. Workers of similar calibre were needed for the making of Horsham slabs; anyone who could cut and fit that stone earned top wages. I have found no record of the Star's medieval menus, but whatever the food was like, accommodation was first class.

The carvings depict scenes to please pilgrim taste: an intrepid saint vanquishes a dragon (divine backing is indicated — his sword has grown to twice the length of its scabbard); there are stolid monkish faces, serpents to be fought, and 'IHS' devoutly carved upon one of the indoor timbers.

Alfriston Star: hostelry for members of medieval package tours

A later embellishment was a ship's figurehead, now standing outside the inn. A remnant of an eighteenth-century wreck, it was probably thought a suitable acquisition for what had been a travellers' hostelry, though the pilgrim trade had ceased long before.

Another house crowned by Horsham slabs narrowly escaped destruction in 1944. St Mary's, Bramber, dated from the fourteenth century. It had a varied life, having been owned by the distinguished Knights Templar in its early days. They were succeeded by Benedictines. Later, it is said that the future Charles II sheltered there during his flight to France, though so many places claim that distinction that one tends to bracket them with those in which Elizabeth Tudor slept. However, the claim of St Mary's is more credible than some, for in addition to its fifteen rooms it is said to have a few secret passages, including one connecting it with Bramber Castle at the other end of the village.

By the close of the Second World War the house was in a parlous state, and little interest was shown when it was offered at auction, except by one lady and a firm of builders.

That firm sounded an echo from six centuries ago. The Horsham house in 1357 was demolished for its stones; St Mary's was going to be demolished for the sake of its timbers. One lady had decided otherwise, and managed to outbid her opponents. Having done that, Miss Dorothy Ellis faced an acute shortage of money, in addition to the then prevalent shortages of materials and labour. She adopted a gradual approach.

Patient saving was the only way to ensure that ancient timbers and Horsham slabs would in due course be expertly restored; meanwhile Miss Ellis's own artistry was put to use indoors. Painted wooden panelling and leather wall-hangings dating from the time of the first Elizabeth needed time and delicacy; outside, the grounds were in similar state. Years of labour lay ahead.

Now, St Mary's is a splendid sight; standing sideways to the main street of Bramber, it faces a small but elegant garden noted for its topiary, and the Spanish gates which are more like black lace than wrought iron. It is recognized as one of the country's best timber-framed buildings, yet we came so near to losing it.

English people have a great reputation as pet-lovers, but often enough the pets, rather than being four-footed and furry, tend to have walls and windows. Look in the yellow pages, most volumes, most districts. There, in profusion, are do-it-yourself shops for the home-lover with an independent streak; and building firms, large, small and in between, thronging and thriving. They will design, build, extend, renovate; wish-fulfilment is their business.

Even so, no one offers to transplant an entire house from one county to the next, grafting it onto another dwelling already *in situ*. It seems not to be a procedure in great demand. Those of us who groan at the prospect of Moving House are in fact groaning only at the prospect of Moving Furniture – enough cause for groaning, in all conscience, but hardly bearing comparison with the real thing.

Nathaniel Lloyd did exactly that. His family home, Dixter Manor, was an impressive fifteenth-century house with a massively beamed medieval hall and a solar with the original fireplace. To this splendour he added a complete house from Benenden, just across the border in Kent. It dated from the sixteenth century, but also had a medieval-style hall; smaller, but perfect in conjunction with its older partner. Members of Sussex Archaeological Society, in the summer of 1932, were shown around and duly impressed: 'The house is surrounded by a beautiful garden, forming a fitting setting . . .'

No wonder the Society secretary was somewhat lost for words. Mr Lloyd's son was a gardener of similar standard to Gertrude Jekyll, and they had worked on it together, guided by Lutyens.

Dixter is only one of the great houses in Northiam village; at the opposite end there is Brickwall, of vintage similar to Dixter's but with a number of later additions. Between them stands the house which is said to be the smallest in England – that is, the smallest two-storey house; overall, about the size of a potting shed. There is an old photograph from forty years ago, when its doll's-house door and window were boarded up, and the little chimney pointed skywards as if trying to catch attention. Even so, the brickwork was plainly no amateur effort, and the tiling was in fair condition. At one time a family of five lived there,

The smallest house in Northiam – Smugglers' Cottage

though they were surely flyweights. The mansard roof allows as much headroom as possible upstairs; at ground level, one can only suppose that at least one person sat on the stairs, deb-fashion. Now it is beautifully tended, and named 'Smugglers' Cottage' – though it would have contributed little to the welfare of those gentlemen. It belongs to a neighbouring householder, and probably delights his weekend guests. Its origins are mysterious; from the quality of the workmanship, it seems akin to the follies specially ordered to give employment to good workmen. But Northiam is only a short distance from Peasmarsh; Peasmarsh Place was the Liddell home.

Liddell? Alice Lidell. Alice in Wonderland . . . perhaps a gift for a child who loved that story; perhaps a child who knew Alice.

Also on the way to Brickwall there is that village green where the prisoner in the blind house was caught as he wriggled out, during a short sermon. There is another thing too. It is not of architectural interest, but when one can say 'Elizabeth Tudor picnicked here', instead of 'Elizabeth Tudor slept here', it is not a chance to be missed. She did so beneath an oak tree which is now so old, so massive, that it could well collapse from exhaustion, but every effort is made to preserve that tree in memory of one sunny August day four centuries ago. Imagine the splendid, heavy-eyed lady, imperious, looking less than her thirty-nine years, accepting the adoration of gaping locals as her everyday due, tasting the food hurried out to her from the inn, which is still there. Like Elizabeth that day, it shows little sign of the passing years; like Brickwall.

This is not the sort of name Englishmen tend to give the homes they love, yet there are two in Sussex: this, in Northiam, and another in Sedlescombe. Perhaps the seventeenth-century iron master, newly wealthy, who built his smaller mansion, was imitating the earlier specimen which needed no evocative name to give it consequence. It stood foursquare, facing the high wrought iron gates, and bearing little resemblance to Dixter; though each century brought further additions, the primly symmetrical façade survived. The Frewen family had owned it for centuries, among them an archbishop and other prominent citizens – most of them the friends of the royal House, hence the visit of Elizabeth Tudor. When a house first appeared on that site, perhaps its walls, partly brick-built, seemed rather grand if surrounded mostly by cottages of wattle and daub. As the house and its occupants grew in grandeur and importance, the name seemed more workaday. It was of no consequence.

This layered architecture, which presents a fairly mature face to the world but hides progressively older layers beneath, is not rare; there is an interesting example in Steyning. To reach it, walk along Church Street to the corner on which stands Saxon Cottage; a purely medieval timber framed and thatched little dwelling which attempts its fraud so charmingly that one pats the gatepost and passes along. Let it play Saxon if it likes – maybe the name of the builder, or the first owner, was Saxon.

The largest house in Northiam – Brickwall

Turn the corner: pass – if you can – another house with a splendid roof of Horsham slabs; there, standing back a little from the road, is Chantry House, with a symmetrical, sedate, serene Georgian front which speaks peace and comfort as convincingly as anything in all this world. But peel off a layer of that house and you come to the Stuart layer, from about 1625. Beneath that comes the Tudor layer, and there the peace and comfort stop. Because it was to Chantry Green, that pretty patch of turf still facing Chantry House and in full view, that they brought one of the Protestant martyrs in the time of Mary Tudor. There he was tied to the stake for the supreme sacrifice, just as Catholics had suffered not so long before under Henry, and as they would suffer again. Chantry House witnessed unforgettable misery.

Yet if we replace the layers – the Stuart, then the Georgian, so that the house is again as we now know it, we have the place in which the poet Yeats delighted to spend holidays with friends. Was it here that he wrote that most moving of poems –

Had I the heavens' embroidered cloths,
Enwrought with golden and silver light,
The blue and the dim and the dark cloths
Of night and light and the half light,
I would spread the cloths under your feet:
But I, being poor, have only my dreams;
I have spread my dreams under your feet:
Tread softly, because you tread on my dreams.

An absolution, and a healing.

Ashcombe Toll House – precursor of traffic wardens and tax discs

A very different house is still in its old place beside the Lewes – Brighton road, at the junction of Kingston Lane. A circular house, with a smoothly rounded roof; one's first thought is that it might be a blind house, but the site is wrong. This is a tollhouse, and the keeper lived in that cramped dwelling, collecting the small fees from passing travellers. He seems to have had a marked lack of mod cons – or indeed of any cons whatever. It was a shelter, and a living of sorts; tolls were never a popular imposition. Heathfield poultrymen taking birds to market at some distance from home used to take their carts as far as their local tollhouse just before midnight, and wait. As the church clock chimed, they moved forward, paid their toll and were away. One payment covered them for twenty-four hours; if they went without dawdling, they could get to market and back for the one fee. No doubt the keeper of the round tollhouse dealt regularly with similarly economically minded tradesmen. There was no escaping him, for the house had two windows, though what happened when he fell asleep was something else entirely – unless he had a wife or a paid assistant. Ashcombe Toll House is only a small building but it houses a fair-sized question mark.

So do three other round buildings; the churches at Southease, Piddinghoe and Lewes. Each has a round tower; they are the only ones in the whole county, all in the same river valley – the Ouse – and very close together. Various reasons have been suggested for their occurrence; it is likely that Piddinghoe and Southease were intended for use as watch-towers. Much has been heard of English depredation in France, but the French terrorized south-east England for many years, and when the Ouse was so far navigable that Lewes was a port, vigilance was essential. Of those two churches, Piddinghoe was beside the river, just where it came out of one sharp bend and went into another; just where enemy boats would have to slacken speed a little. Southease, further upstream, was set a little back from the water but with a clear view of a long, straight stretch. One small basis for doubt is the lack of slits (oillets) in Southease tower. Piddinghoe is well supplied, and their position emphasizes their purpose, but if the theory applies to Southease, it must at some time have had oillets which were later obscured.

The round tower in Lewes, at St Michael's Church, dates from the thirteenth century – about a century younger than the others.

It seems less likely to have been intended as a watch-tower, as the castle was on much higher ground, with an excellent view of the river; it may have been erected by the builder responsible for the round towers of the castle, which also date from that time.

Smaller churches served as watch-towers, sanctuaries and places of worship, and their ancient fabric is, in most cases, as sturdy as ever. Yet the greatest church in Sussex, Chichester Cathedral, has several times been destroyed or damaged by fire; it has always risen from the ashes – a phoenix cathedral.

Its long life did not begin in Chichester. In the seventh century St Wilfrid came from his See of York and found famine. The inhabitants of Selsey were starving; first, he taught them to be fishermen, then he taught them to be Christians. Their king gave him land. There the cathedral was built, and it served for several centuries until the arrival of the Normans, who moved the See to the former Roman town, Chichester. The deserted cathedral built by St Wilfrid stood in the path of the encroaching sea. How much now remains, deeply submerged, is unknown, but stones appear from time to time, and legends live on.

The Norman building was soon under way, but after a mere thirty-nine years' work a fire destroyed much of the effort so far expended. That was in 1114, but even greater efforts restored the whole cathedral after only nine more years. After little more than half a century's work, another fire wrecked the roof timbers and much of the building with them.

The phoenix rose from the flames; it also arose from the flames of controversy through the centuries. The bishop during the Reformation was Robert Sherbourne. Opinion is divided as to whether he was wise, or merely wily; but he brought his bishopric safely through that difficult period – an achievement which is at least eloquent of keen intelligence.

A century later, the Puritans were even more difficult to cope with than Henry VIII; there were far more of them, and they lacked his respect for books and manuscripts. Roof timbers had been replaced after conflagration; ancient books on a bonfire had gone for ever, though the library was subsequently restocked by generous donors.

Curiously, a shrine which in medieval days was one of the main centres of pilgrimage, has become the focal point for modern pilgrims. St Richard was bishop for only eight years during the thirteenth century, and his tomb was despoiled by Henry VIII, but of late it has regained its place in people's affections.

Other focal points in the cathedral are still embellished by treasures; not the precious stones of olden days, but frequently treasures of modern art; tapestries, stained glass, metalwork and embroidery. Most vividly, the kinship between past and present is demonstrated by an enterprise which was started about twenty years ago. The maintenance of ancient buildings brings in ever-increasing bills; the latter half of the twentieth century is the fund-raisers' nightmare. Chichester Cathedral founded its own firm, and its own school for craftsmen; not just another corner within the cathedral complex – suitable premises were taken on an industrial estate. There, workmen with the necessary skills – joiners, stonemasons and metalworkers among others – train young workers to follow in their footsteps. They are in constant demand all over the country, repairing and reconstructing ancient buildings, sacred and secular. This phoenix rises every day.

Cathedrals, abbeys, priories, churches; all were religious establishments, all devoted to prayer and charitable works. Yet they were hated. It was Offa's fault; he of the Dyke, and the eighth century.

From early times those establishments had been entitled to the tax known as tithes; a tenth of income from agriculture of industry, from the rich or poor. Initially it had been a moral obligation; one of those things which could be avoided if a man put his mind to it – not as a regular practice, but when necessary. Offa, keen to ingratiate himself with the Pope, made them compulsory, and it was only a matter of time – one and a half centuries – before the Church was able to make non-payment punishable by excommunication. There was a heavy price to pay for so great an access of wealth. Buildings had to be provided to house the tithes paid in kind, such as farming produce. Barns were built on Church property, and when possible they were burned down; preferably when full. As the population increased so did the volume of receipts; many barns needed to be larger. There still had to be smaller barns to contain the odd assortment

Alciston: one of the largest tithe barns in England

which parish priests received as tithes; Sussex folk had an old saying, defining anything insatiable: 'Like the parson's barn – it takes in everything'! In Sussex, at Alciston, there stands one of the greatest tithe barns in the whole country. It was one of the properties of Battle Abbey which owned vast estates; Alciston was a sort of outpost of empire to which far-flung taxpayers might deliver their tithes. Pay As You Earn, with the added sting of Do It Yourself delivery.

Looking at that great barn, 170 feet long, built in the fourteenth century when tithes had proliferated beyond the wildest nightmares of Offa's contemporaries, one can imagine the bitterness of peasants after a poor season. A tenth, even of the little their land had yielded, to be relinquished, and added to the vast store already held by those fat monks. Many monks were spare, devout men dedicated to their calling; the care of the sick and the beggars, the education of boys in their schools; but tithes were a pervasive, distorting bitterness for which even the Reformation brought no relief. Ecclesiastical estates merely passed to laymen – people currently in royal favour. Tithes were still compulsory;

they were payable to the Church of England or local lords instead of Rome. True, those barns must be built, and there was great work for craftsmen – foresters, woodmen, carpenters, masons, smiths, tilers, bricklayers – but even then the barns were there only to be filled; a culmination of the craftsmen's arts and the peasants' misery.

For the ordinary clergy they were an acute embarrassment, well into the nineteenth century. Priests were often younger sons of gentry, with their own incomes as well as their stipends and tithes, and the latter were as legally binding upon recipients as the donors. There is a Sussex story of one such unfortunate who hit upon the idea of an annual tithe dinner to sweeten the atmosphere; the Tithe Feast, for all who were in any way concerned. The rector sat at the top table, doing honour to the occasion in his best tail coat. Nervous of causing ill feeling, he drank with anyone who cared to ask him, and was eventually carried home. Those who carried him chopped off his coat tails, propped him against the rectory door, pulled the bell and ran – but not so far that they missed the crash as his wife opened the door.

Poorer clergy endured other humiliations. Some depended upon tithes in kind; a resentful farmer would leave every tenth sheaf standing, spread out over acres of farmland. If the weather were unkind, some at least would rot before the clergyman could collect so scattered a harvest.

We may admire a tithe barn, revering its age and the skill of the builders, but there will always be a chill remembrance of the attendant circumstances.

Go to Wilmington Priory and be comforted. Its properties were never so well cared for as those of Battle Abbey, and the barn was left to deteriorate through the centuries. A few years ago it had to be dismantled except for the lower part of the walls. They still surround what was the ancient floor of the barn, a space now used as a car park. A modern peasant may position his Cadillac-type pride and joy with a feeling of satisfaction – a modest revenge, though it may cost him a few pence in the parking meter. Just a tithe or two.

North of Lewes, there is a very small tithe barn, which was built for the use of the rectors of Chailey. Half-way between the village church and the rectory, its official date is about 1600, but the oldest surviving timbers, the wall plate and side posts, are silvered with age and as hard as sarsen stone. In short, they have the same appearance and density as timbers of the twelfth century or thereabouts. The upper timbers, with the tiling and brickwork, seem on brief examination to be more recent. It is as though the original barn was on at least one occasion reduced to the wall plates and side posts, and rebuilt from there.

This view is supported by the rectory, only a short walk away and visible through the trees. This is one of the oldest of Sussex rectories, and the only moated example. Folk memory, so surprisingly reliable, says that the moat was dug by one of the rectors in self-defence. In proportion to the house, it is deep and wide; though no Bodiam, the rectory was well protected from a shock attack by country folk, though perhaps not from the more skilful military men who led soldiers on both sides during the Civil War.

The moat was, and is, fed by Longford stream, flowing from the north of the parish; one wonders whether at any time the stream was diverted, depriving the rectory of its protection. It may have been entirely on glebe land, though even then there was little to prevent trespassers damming it after dusk.

The house is another layered building. Its recorded date is 1600; therefore in its early form it was planned in the late sixteenth century and was being built during the last year or so of that century. An eighteenth-century occupant added an outer shell in the Georgian style, enlarging the house and completely changing its appearance. At the same time, he was an historically minded man, foreseeing the interest of future generations in his new layer of parsonage. Whilst matching the wood of the indoor panelling, he left his new panels plain; one can see clearly where the old house ended and his later addition began. It is almost as if he is still delighted to show the interested visitor around.

In 1964 the moat was dredged, and a quantity of broken tobacco-pipes were found. They were thought to date from the mid-eighteenth century; probably the discarded aids to concentration belonging to the workmen who built the Georgian layer.

Perforce, Chailey incumbents had to collect their tithes, filling the barn and in later days taking the statutory 'commutation' – money instead of payment in kind. Doubtless many a priest by

Chailey Moat: peace at last

quiet labour and strength of character overcame personal bitterness, but in our own century the Jellicoe family of Chailey produced a son who was to make spectacular restitution – if indeed any were necessary.

Basil Jellicoe was the rector's son, and it was planned that after Oxford he would enter the priesthood. As he grew up, he inclined towards Anglo-Catholicism. To a young man brought up in the exquisite moated rectory and the academic peace of Oxford, the slums of London came as an icy shock during his first curacy. In his mid-twenties he led a mission near St Pancras; he was quite as capable of wielding a scrubbing brush as of uttering soothing words. He did what was needed where it was needed as soon as he saw the necessity, and it happened constantly. Vigorously, he campaigned for slum-clearance – not tirelessly, for after a few years he was a sick man. For a while he disregarded medical opinion, but when he collapsed he was forced to recuperate in Sussex.

As a convalescent, Jellicoe ought to have enjoyed walks in Chailey and the surrounding countryside, but he found poverty there too: beautiful Sussex had farm labourers living in hovels on starvation wages, and unemployment was a familiar spectre even in the prettiest villages. It was not the most sensible way to rest and recover, but Father Jellicoe founded a housing association, dedicated to St Richard. It built, or created out of existing buildings, decent homes for people who had never been so privileged. Within a year there were five groups of homes, both flats and cottages; it all depended upon the current most pressing need, and the current provision available. He travelled, he preached, he pleaded and begged, and the response was good; people warmed to him and his cause, which expanded and prospered. At the age of thirty-six the founder died.

Though the Anglo-Catholic Church does not confer sainthood, the reverence with which Basil Jellicoe is remembered, half a century after his death, is the equivalent. 'Christ's most precious gift' – so he was described. That beautiful rectory where he was born seems specially designed for children – corridors and corners, steps up and steps down; the perfect place for hide-and-seek. That moat is no bad place for sailing boats. The little dark boy, the future saint, enjoyed his childhood there.

The house ceased to be a rectory long since; it was too expensive for the incumbent to maintain. Here endeth the fat parson, battening on the ill-gotten contents of his tithe barn. Since then, Chailey Rectory has become Chailey Moat, neither a liability nor an embarrassment but a private place, loved by its owners. And the tithe barn rests in peace – Garden Shed Extraordinary.

The story of Chailey Moat is that of a political and pastoral time-bomb, even though it does have a happy ending. Castle Goring has no hassle, no heartache, no humiliation – just glorious slapstick.

At present it houses a college for students from all over the world; as many languages are heard on the Goring campus as on that other campus in the Old Testament – the one at Babel – and Castle Goring is an architectural Tower of Babel. The building itself may be excused on grounds of extreme youth; as late as 1790, it was barely a twinkle in its owner's eye. He and his architect were known respectively as Shelley and Rebecca – names to rejoice the hearts of any modern pop duo; in fact they

Castle Goring, by Shelley and Rebecca...

were an English baronet and an Italian architect. A male Italian architect. Between them, they contrived to erect a purists' nightmare.

Its present position is just south of the A27 on the way to Worthing; travelling east, you can either turn left to visit Justice Shelley and family in Clapham church, or go straight ahead, with an occasional glance to your right. Through the trees you will see a splendid Gothic castle – towers, battlements, all complete.

Too complete. The fun begins when you examine it accompanied by one of those little guide-books which tell you all about architecture; what the well-heeled Norman was living in when William the Bastard reigned, or during the tenure of subsequent monarchs when architecture passed through the Norman, Early English, Decorated and Perpendicular variations of the Gothic style.

Castle Goring might appear to have been built by ghosts – ghosts with a Dickensian flavour, for it was he who invented not only the Ghost of Christmas Past but also the Ghost of

. . . or Rebecca and Shelley

Christmas to Come. Here, a ghost from Hastings days hovered round for 300 years or so, in order to watch a late-medieval mason carving, with the finest chisels, a softly arched window graduating to a gentle point; then the ghost swung his hefty hammer and mighty chisel and knocked out a good strong dog-tooth ornament around the outer edge. It was worth the long wait.

Or was it the Hastings man who had first go, making a typically rounded Norman arch? The Ghost of Perps To Come hovered – possibly with some impatience; it would be impossible to execute the delicate carving around his lancet window (next in line along the wall) when every blow from that ungainly fellow shook the whole edifice to its foundations.

There were of course no ghosts, but Shelley and Rebecca did the job very well in spite of such deprivation. Perhaps some errant gene disported itself within Sir Bysshe Shelley's soul; he was a distant relative of Justice Shelley in Clapham church, he of the downtrodden mien and anxious countenance. If so, no gene ever had such jollifications, as is proved by the other side of

Castle Goring: the south-facing side provides the best transformation scene in the whole of show business. Officially it is Graeco-Palladian; in fact, it is watered-down White House; not so aggressively whitewashed – the glare is relieved by delicate colour tones here and there, and the size is less film set, more human habitation. Which is curious indeed, because it is said that no Shelley ever lived there.

Probably there was more than a modicum of keeping up with the Georgian Joneses. When Castle Goring was first discussed, in 1790, a fine house further along the road to the east was well on its way and already showing signs of as much changeability as the weather. The Marine Pavilion at Brighton had been complete, according to the plans by Henry Holland, for three years. Rebecca had painted the wall panels and ceiling of the elegant Saloon; he had been to various other great houses, designing and decorating. By the time Shelley caught up with him, he had probably developed a prima donna streak – if indeed he had not been born with it – but he was a status symbol, the fashionable man to employ. While the Marine Pavilion went on its dazzling way, soon to become the Royal Pavilion, Sir Bysshe Shelley, with one of its artists in his own employ, was unlikely to do much to upset the creative muse, even if he was rather chary of taking up residence.

Subsequent generations had little chance. A son died in his late twenties; the poet grandson, Percy Bysshe Shelley, was drowned at the age of twenty-nine. Being so young, he might well have changed his radical opinions later, but his stricture on the Royal Pavilion was clear enough: 'a bauble'. Would a mature poet have taken to the slapstick castle after all, perhaps delighting in its perversity?

Castle Goring: two halves of a house, combined in one enjoyable whole like an angel cake. Tucked away in the Cuckmere Valley, all alone among the trees, is half a church. As the seagull flies, it is barely half a mile from busy Alfriston, thronging with visitors anxious to see the Clergy House, the Cathedral of the Downs and all the other wonders. Yet Lullington church seems to be alone in the world, and at least a quarter of a mile away from the nearest house, Lullington Court.

It is said, rather too often, that this is claimed to be the smallest church in Britain. There is a commercially produced picture postcard which describes Lullington as the smallest church in England, but the church's own leaflet says simply that it is one of the smallest in the country.

That claim is unassailable. It is sixteen feet square, seating twenty people comfortably, but on special occasions like Christmas it will take almost twice that number.

It is known to date from the thirteenth century and though at first the property of the abbot of Battle it was soon transferred to Chichester, where the current bishop was St Richard. As the original dedication is uncertain, perhaps some day Lullington might be re-dedicated to St Richard who once owned it. In the past it was certainly much larger. What remains is only part of the chancel; old foundations were excavated twenty years ago, and it seems possible that the destruction took place in Cromwellian times.

The distance between the church and the nearest village may seem curious at first sight but there are similar instances in Sussex and elsewhere; church and village were originally together, but when the Black Death came, villagers moved away from the contaminated spot, built new homes and left an isolated church. It may well have happened here.

Not until 1806 was the church repaired and made fit for use. A quarter of a mile away – much nearer than Litlington village – stood the big house, Lullington Court; such residences often had a private chapel somewhere in the grounds, shared by the family, their servants, and any interested villagers and neighbours. This little church was just the right size for such use. Further repairs were done in 1894; one assumes that it had been in regular use during that century. Though charming, it is curious: no one has certain knowledge about its dedication, when or why it was devastated, or why it stands in solitary beauty.

Early in the 1930s an architect in Sussex was employed in the task of building a replica of Lullington church in the USA, as a war memorial. Which architect, which state and for whom – no one seems to know. Curious, but one hopes that they also made a replica of the surroundings. It may be only half a church, but standing as it does, almost hidden in such a beautiful place, it is a haven of tranquillity.

Half a church at Lullington

Battle Abbey was not. William founded it as a thank-offering for the Hastings victory. Built on part of the battlefield, with the altar reputedly on the spot where Harold fell, doubtless its counterpart would have been there had the roles of victor and vanquished been reversed. Following William's intentions, it became a thriving house of Benedictines, well run, exceedingly well endowed, and an asset to the people for many miles around; an ecclesiastical People's Welfare Centre in spite of the hated tithes.

Then came Henry VIII and the Dissolution of the Monasteries. Battle Abbey was a plum ripe for picking, and Sir Anthony Browne was the man with the basket; a favourite of the King, and he had the somewhat unusual knack of keeping that status. Not only Battle Abbey but all its vast estates went to Sir Anthony. His already overweening self-importance was inflated, and his manner of turning the monks out of the abbey was abrasive in the extreme. One old man, weary and humiliated beyond endurance, cursed Browne as he left: the last of his family would perish by fire and water.

It was somewhat unsatisfactory from the monk's point of view; procrastination was hardly adequate to the anguish of the moment. But his glimpse of the future was correct, even though 2½ centuries were to pass before the curse took effect. Sir Anthony, the real villain, lived on in wealth and comfort, becoming Viscount Montague. Battle Abbey was converted into a luxurious mansion; he also owned Cowdray Castle, a splendid house at Midhurst. Built only at the end of the fifteenth century, it came to him from his half-brother, another of Henry's favourites. Nothing went amiss for the new Viscount.

By 1793 his descendants may well have forgotten the curse. They perhaps enjoyed a little superior amusement at the efforts of Shelley and Rebecca at Castle Goring which had been in progress for three years, but there was also some building work on hand at home. Cowdray needed repair, but the Viscount went abroad and was put to no inconvenience.

The men working on the south wing left a fire unattended. When the resultant inferno had done its worst, the kitchen remained unharmed but the rest of the castle was a shell. Contents beyond price were reduced to ashes. Just over a week later, the Viscount, in Germany, was drowned. He had no son.

No one has lived there since. Temporary owners used a lodge on the estate; they lost two sons at sea. In Victorian times, a mansion was built on the estate, but just out of sight of the castle, which is still preserved as it was after the fire, as being of historical interest. Battle Abbey is in similar case; neither mansion nor abbey, it is a focal point for tourists, though part of it houses a school. Of historical interest only.

Medieval Rye must also have felt itself to be under a curse; the inhabitants perished by fire, water and the French.

The latter were not being merely piratical. In the early thirteenth century, English barons, trying to depose King John, went so far as to invite the French royal heir to take over the English crown. Unexpectedly, John died, and the barons changed their minds. The French were not so obliging, and vented their feelings in many raids; there were sea battles and coastline assaults. At that time Rye was still a port, and raiders could sail right up to it for the attack. Which they did.

John's son, Henry III, gave orders for a small castle to be built for the town's defence. Thirty-five feet square, it had a tower at each corner, with stout walls about four feet thick. Even so, walls were still desperately needed around the town for adequate protection, and they were hardly complete before the raids intensified. They increased in ferocity, until in 1377 there was a raid of overwhelming terror. The mini-castle, Baddings Tower, was not enough; the town walls had to be rebuilt completely.

When finished, they were much stronger and included a fortification known as the Land Gate. Sixty feet wide, it had twin towers joined by a double arch and portcullis; the French never got the better of that. Baddings Tower was put to use as a temporary town hall until the one destroyed by the French could be replaced. Meanwhile, the sea took over the serious business of defence; by throwing up gravel, it silted up the harbour, making attacks very risky. The smaller tower has long been known as the Ypres Tower, having been sold to John de Ypres for private use, after the French threat dwindled. It was soon re-purchased by the town, and has been many things – prison, soup kitchen, morgue and now museum.

One more look at the Land Gate shows a curious point. Of the two arches, the inner and outer, one is of an earlier shape with a more pointed arch; the other has the eliptical arch of the later Perpendicular period. At first sight, the mixture looks like a foreshadowing of the antics of Shelley and Rebecca. However, the Land Gate was reinforced some years after the initial building; no doubt the later craftsmen incorporated some newfangled notions.

Blue Dick and Dowsing: two vandals with but a single thought. They went their ways, one from Canterbury and one from East Anglia, but both with the same mission and the same method. They carried hammers and they smashed all the stained glass they could find in all the windows of all the churches they could manage to visit.

They lived during the Commonwealth in the time of Oliver Cromwell: the common weal did not extend to people with opinions different from their own. They and their aides worked a busy way through all the popish glass they could find, and that included a vast amount in Sussex, which had been particularly rich in medieval stained glass.

Such enthusiasm was occasionally self-defeating. So intent were they upon smashing large areas of glass that sometimes higher and smaller windows escaped their attention. Which is why it is wise, when entering any ancient Sussex church, to remember the words 'I will lift up mine eyes'. You may be lucky.

High in the east window of North Stoke there is a dainty example showing the coronation of the Virgin Mary. Burpham has a Flemish roundel. Near the gate of Pevensey Castle, Westham church has, in the east window, a medieval picture of saints and apostles, each carrying an appropriate symbol: Peter has keys, James a pilgrim's staff, and Andrew a cross. Matthew has a carpenter's square.

The ancient craft of the carpenter is brought to mind when one looks at the lychgate of Bramber church. Its supports have the distinctive curve of cruck timbers, and the silver-grey glint which goes with great age. I asked the firm who, some thirty years since, had been responsible for the work; the supports were recorded as made of salvaged material, but there were no other details.

Crucks were oak; trunks, or main branches, split (not sawn) into two equal parts – a task for experts only – and used

Missed by the Puritans – medieval glass at Westham

symmetrically as supports for roofs or timber-framed buildings. In houses they were usually gable ends. In great buildings such as farm barns, tithe barns and churches, whole trunks of the very largest trees were used, and they supported the most ponderous weights for many centuries.

The crucks at Bramber are not of those mighty dimensions, but perhaps more sturdy than those in timber-framed houses, and they have no trace of the black pigment which usually protects house timbers. During the Civil War, Cromwell's men, in taking Bramber Castle from the Royalists, almost destroyed the adjacent Norman church. Afterwards, the nave was repaired, but not until the late eighteenth century could anything be done to restore the wrecked chancel and tower. There were no endowments; money was lacking, so some of the materials from the chancel ruins were perforce used to restore the tower. There was therefore no chancel remaining.

But were there a few timbers left? Timbers from an Early English chancel, bearing the silver-grey tinge of great age? It seems possible that they now grace the beautiful lychgate which is also the war memorial of the ancient church.

Even more ancient is the church at Sompting – at the very

Ancient timbers in Bramber lychgate

least, a century older than Bramber, and a Saxon masterpiece. A grey stone building like no other in England, with a cap of darker shade, shaped like a Rhenish helm – seen frequently in the Rhineland but unique in England. It was there complete, standing and functioning, more than a century before that doleful writer recorded in the Anglo-Saxon Chronicle that Harold 'was informed that William the Bastard was about to invade this land ... King Harold gathered together a great host and came to oppose him at the grey apple tree ... there was great slaughter on both sides.'

And while great slaughter took its toll within sight of the grey apple tree, a day's ride away to the west the grey-hooded church, already old, was open as a sanctuary for those who feared the outcome.

Another grey building, in Midhurst, was built many centuries

St Mary's, Bramber: the life work of Dorothy Ellis

later. It is a trim Georgian house, with its name neatly carved on the stone lintel: 'The Old Savings Bank'.

Such establishments were opened in Sussex in the early nineteenth century. They were popular; between 1812 and 1819 there were at least nine positioned fairly evenly through the county. The guarantors were not exactly philanthropists, but they were generous. There were usually four to each bank, and without their backing such banks could not have been established. They were particularly for the use of small depositors: domestic servants, minors, tradesmen, artisans – people whose deposits would normally be too small for consideration. In the early days, five per cent interest was paid as soon as a deposit reached the sum of £1, though no account was allowed to exceed £50. However, following the Napoleonic period and the onset of depression, interest was perforce reduced to four per cent. It was still good value.

So many buildings, ancient and not so ancient, large and small, and for varied purposes; what of the trimming on top? In this

Pyecombe church, with its own welcoming pastoral symbol

county where the tradition of ironwork is strong, many buildings have weathervanes, lovingly wrought. They are not confined to church towers; neither have they much to do with the weather. In a world where weather forecasts appear regularly on radio and television, and on demand by telephone, weathervanes are simply decorative, and they can be very attractive.

They were once a symbol of honour. Royal permission was needed to erect one elsewhere than on a church, and that permission had to be earned. The earliest known specimen in England is a curious mixture. Made of copper, not brass, it shows the family crest of the local squires, the Echynghams of Etchingham. Though it is their crest, the weathervane is on the church, for the family paid for its re-building during the fourteenth century

At Rushlake Green some flats for elderly people have a most attractive modern vane in wrought-iron filigree, made in the 1960s by a local smith. The architects of some new buildings in Waterloo Place, Lewes, designed an appropriate symbol: a silhouette of the Iron Duke, mounted on a charger, sword at the ready – made also by a local smith. Older vanes were not always gilded cockerels. At Rye church one was cut in the letters 'AR' with the date 1703 – it was placed there in the year after Queen Anne's accession. Crawley, where flooding is not unknown, has a dove with an olive branch flying above the church – shades of Noah and his Ark. The old Christian symbol of a fish is quite common: the churches of St John the Baptist, in Lewes, and Piddinghoe, just to the south, have fish vanes, reminding people of the stories of Jesus and his fishermen disciples. The cockerel is a reminder to be watchful.

One last curious thing. Sussex, once an ironworking county and now with strong resurgence of the craft; Sussex, wherein the smiths made shepherds' crooks by the score for the Downland shepherds' use; where the smith at Pyecombe made the Pyecombe hook, best-beloved implement of shepherds born and bred; where that smith now has a busy trade in those Pyecombe hooks, not for shepherds but mainly for bishops as part of their regalia: a splendid example adorns the gate of Pyecombe church. But it seems that no one has used that very Sussex, pastoral symbol as part of a church weathervane. Curious.

7   Mainly Horticultural

Go to Brighton, to Preston Park. There is an arched gateway within which the gate is the summit of the art of Sussex blacksmiths. A Spanish mantilla, cobwebby, lighter than air, has been transformed into metal but only as a temporary measure: at any moment it must sink softly to the grass. It is work of rare artistry, a delight.

That delight shows in visitors' faces as they trace its fine tendrils with gentle fingers before they go on, into the garden, where all the plants are scented. Flowers, foliage and herbs – all were chosen for their perfume. Lilac, rosemary, lavender, heliotrope, sweet pea, wallflower and many different varieties of roses and herbs. Mint alone numbered at least eight kinds at the last count.

Beside the garden paths there are guide rails with plant labels in Braille, for this is a garden planned specially for the blind. It was started in the early spring of 1953 as part of Brighton's celebrations for Coronation Year, and the idea aroused great enthusiasm. There were many contributions and gifts – eight teak garden seats arrived from various donors almost as soon as the first announcement was made – and the local butchers gave a summerhouse in which visitors might shelter whilst enjoying the extra fragrance of a garden in the rain.

Later in the same year, Hove made a similar haven in St Anne's Well Gardens. The paths were laid with loose gravel so that the approach of other visitors was audible, though more gentle sounds came from a small dovecote where a pair of Barbary doves made their home. Here, shelter was provided by a pergola; an oak lychgate, roofed with tiles from an old barn, was hardly large enough to shelter more than one or two people, but the feel of the Sussex oak gave great pleasure. It still does. Both gardens flourished and are loved and enjoyed by blind and sighted people alike. One of the blind enthusiasts at Hove asked hesitantly for just one thing more. The sound of running water.

More than thirty years have passed since the first visitors

walked in those gardens. I would like to return late one evening, when the air is warm after a summer shower. The fragrance would be pleasing to the point of rapture. The moths . . .

Moths? According to legend, moths in a garden are the souls of its former lovers. In the scented dusk they return, velvet-winged, to the place they loved best.

I stood in pouring rain, in the oldest garden in England; it was broad daylight, but that detracted not one scrap from the dream-like atmosphere. Not many yards distant, traffic roared along the A27, but it seemed to have receded – not miles, but centuries away.

Almost twenty centuries. This garden, with its palace, came into being about AD 75; although in our time there seems not to have been any official claim to be the oldest, perhaps at that age it ceases to matter; or maybe something over a millennium of hibernation tends to tarnish the gilt on the horticultural gingerbread. Not for me.

Fishbourne is near the coast between Chichester and Bosham. The palace and garden were built for a wealthy local king who is thought to have ruled with the approval of the Romans, whom he certainly admired. His palace was completely Roman in style; under-floor central heating, mosaic floors, a great hall for formal occasions, internal courtyards – and the garden.

For two centuries life continued normally as the property passed from owner to owner. Parts of the building were demolished, improved, replaced, altered – householders are remarkably similar in their ways whether they own an ancient Roman palace or a modern semi.

Then, the palace was destroyed by fire; whether an enemy attack brought it about, or some Cowdray-type domestic accident, is unknown. The remnants of the walls were taken elsewhere, like Horsham slabs in later centuries. The rest – mosaics, hypocausts and gardens – were abandoned and forgotten until 1960. A workman with an excavator began to dig a trench. He found a palace.

The mosaics were still there; in seventeen centuries some pieces had been lost and others dislodged, but much material was still there. The palace could be re-imagined, reconstructed.

The garden was another story. It lay between the great

entrance hall on the eastern side and the audience chamber opposite; something beautiful, yet very formal and impressive, as a palace garden should be.

Herbs Grown and Used at Fishbourne AD *75 and* AD *1960+*

Angelica	Stems used for tea and soup
Balm	Scented leaves flavoured soup and soft drinks
Basil	Salads and medicinal use
Bay	Flavouring and medicinal
Borage	Flavouring
Burnett	Salads and wine-making
Caraway	Flavouring
Chervil	Flavouring
Chives	Flavouring, salads and soups
Coriander	Flavouring and seasoning
Dill	Pickling
Fennel	Flavouring and sauces
Garlic	Flavouring and medicinal
Horehound	Seasoning and medicinal
Horseradish	Salads, sauces and medicinal
Hyssop	Salads, tea, soup, medicinal
Loveage	Salads, soups, sauces, medicinal
Marjoram	Flavouring
Mint	Flavouring
Rosemary	Flavouring, salads, tea, wine
Rue	Medicinal, sauces
Sage	Seasoning, tea, medicinal
Savory	Flavouring, tea, medicinal
Sorrel	Salads, sauces, soups, medicinal
Tarragon	Flavouring
Thyme	Seasoning
Wormwood	Medicinal

Flowers in the Roman garden: lavender, honeysuckle, japonica, cotoneaster, buddleia, viburnum, sweet briar.

Some features were comparatively easy to trace. Water pipes around the outer perimeter had supplied the fountains, of which some broken marble basins were found nearby. This king's taste had something in common with that of the blind man in Hove. Narrow trenches were dug in regular patterns along the side of the paths; close examination of the soil in the trenches showed that it had been loamy, very different from the indigenous clay. The trenches had been specially prepared for low box hedges, and the exact pattern in which they were originally planted was followed in re-planting.

Horticultural archaeologists were also able to discover, by soil examination, which flowers and herbs had been planted. The Romans were adept in the making of scented gardens, sweet briar and lavender being among their favourite plants. Postholes showed that the generally low, formal garden also provided an attractive background view of trees and bushes, some flowering, others apparently cordon fruit trees.

At the south-east corner of the garden visitors may buy seedlings of twenty-seven different herbs, grown in that same place where they were cultivated so long ago; herbs used by the Romans in cookery and medicine. Southwards, where we now have the A27 and the many houses along each side of it, there was also an informal garden with terraces sloping seawards, and a stream. Full-scale investigations are of course impossible, but that much information has been gained from the limited ground still available for investigation.

To have the formal garden is nothing short of a miracle. It provided herbs, flowers and fruit, and a beautiful setting for the palace. Buried and forgotten for so many centuries, now, thanks to the genius of the archaeologists, it is reborn.

The next item is arboricultural rather than horticultural, but it is of the earth; terrestrial, growing in the soil. It is probably the oldest yew forest in Europe; certainly it is the finest.

Many an ancient church boasts an adjacent yew tree of more than a thousand summers. In Kingley Bottom, as it was known until a century or two ago, there is a whole valley of them; a sort of yew tree Geriatric Ward Supreme – except that these trees appear progressively less geriatric as the years pile up behind them. Instead of merely becoming gnarled, and rotting, yews twine together, combining the strength of several trunks. Though each is still fed by its own root system, the great combined mass above ground is immensely sturdier and mutually supportive. Walking among the ancient trees is like treading upon deep-piled carpet; foliage has dropped for centuries and hardly ever been washed away or soaked by a downpour, for these trees, which combine their trunks at ground level, entwine their branches overhead. The carpet underfoot may feel luxurious but one walks in a hushed, almost sinister viridescent gloom, as though in the temple of some alien and inimical religion. It is an expanding temple, and the outer courts are far more cheerful. The sides of the valley are populated by the multitude of descendants of the old trees below, and they are spreading even further, even to the top of Bow Hill. Kingley Vale provided a considerable amount of the inspiration leading to the foundation of nature reserves; it was one of the first, in 1952.

The oldest trees in the valley are said to have been planted about AD 900, after a great victory by the men of Chichester and the surrounding countryside against the marauding Danes, the Sea Wolves.

The Anglo-Saxon Chronicle tells of the event giving the exact date. It had been a hard year – 894 – with Danes harrying and plundering countrywide: East Anglia, Northumbria, Chester, Wales, Devon . . . 'When the host which had besieged Exeter sailed back on its way home, it harried inland in Sussex near Chichester, but the garrison put them to flight and slew many hundred of them, capturing some of their ships.'

The feelings of the victors may better be judged by reading a little further in the Chronicle, a sad comment in 897: 'The host [Danes], by the mercy of God, had not altogether utterly crushed the English people; but they were much more severely crushed during those three years by murrain and plague, most of all by the fact that many of the best of the King's servants in the land passed away during those three years . . . in this year died Aethelhelm, nine nights before midsummer . . .' What a chill of desolation and despair; what a relief, just that one resounding victory, and how appropriate that weary, grieving people longing only for peace should go inland to the valley, taking with them about sixty yew seedlings. Were they planted in memory of warriors lost in the battle?

Folk memory, taking over from the Chronicle, says that the Saxons did exactly that; furthermore, that the dead Vikings were buried in the four great burial mounds on top of Bow Hill – the

Bronze Age barrows which looked down upon Saxon and Dane just as they now overlook twentieth-century Sussex. And there, many people stop in disbelief. But why? Imagine the Saxon position.

Saxon, with only the thinnest gloss of comparatively recent Christianity; circumstances and ancestry all conspired to make them see only with the eyes of a warrior. When the longboats returned yet again, emotion surged in great waves. First, fury that family and possessions were once more endangered. Second, the swift, fiercely concentrated struggle of the battle. Third – exhaustion, triumph, possibly astonishment. Victory – over the Danes? And one other thing.

In those perilous times, a man's greatest attributes were his skill with his sword arm, his bearing on the battlefield. For many years the Saxons' formative influence had been that of Alfred, that leader who above all others had the soul of a king. He would hang a pillaging Sea Wolf as easily as shooting an arrow into a wild boar, but great courage, in friend or foe, was as gold. Those winged helmets lying scattered near Chichester had belonged to worthy opponents, so worthy that the victory had been too close for comfort. Pagans, perhaps, but warriors; worthy of more than just a piled-up conflagration or a communal pit. What more suitable burial place for such men than those pagan mounds on the summit of the hill? Pagan to pagan, dust to dust. Perhaps just the leaders, as a gesture; the days were too full and too anxious to carry every slain Sea Wolf up that steep hillside.

Folk memory rarely fails us; it may well be that the Bronze Age artefacts in those mounds on Bow Hill have had Viking company through the centuries; very little, for the hard-pressed Saxons would have salvaged anything of use, but some small objects may still remain.

As do the greater ones; those enormous yews of Kingley Vale, still growing and multiplying, and maintaining their own green chapel of remembrance.

From the oldest of forests to an ancient watermill. Look at the Ordnance Survey map, north of Shoreham along the A2037. Just north of Small Dole the main road is crossed by a Roman road; on their junction lies Woods Mill.

Watermills were introduced by the Romans; it is surely more

Woods Mill: from Roman developers to modern conservationists

than coincidence that this watermill is at the confluence of two streams, right beside a Roman road, along which generations of farmers could have brought their crops to the miller.

Though the strongest probability, it can still be only an assumption; however, the Domesday Book records two watermills near Henfield. Again, the Ordnance Survey shows West Mill Farm, to the west of Woods Mill, and tucked between one of the Woods Mill streams and the Roman road. Both mills belonged to Stretham Manor in 1647 (then spelt Streatham), but by 1718 Woods Mill had passed to the Manor of Oram, according to the original deeds. The modern map shows Oreham just to the south of Woods Mill. The lords of both manors had been doing a little business between themselves.

1718 is the date on the deeds of conveyance whereby Richard Lish paid £185 to purchase 'Messuage and water corn mill, outbuildings and three closes, part of the manor of Oram'.

Richard could only make his mark, but it was firm, not one of those shaky crosses usually made by nervous people confronting legal men. He needed to be a strong character, not given to drink or sudden bouts of temper. The mill building, though not deliberately designed for instant retribution, was ideal for that purpose. Each storey of the high building had only half a floor, leaving a damaging plunge to the depths of the wheelpit for the momentarily unwary. Richard worked in that mill for thirty years.

The next owner was William Wood. At first sight the name, Woods Mill, had nothing to do with William, appearing as it did in the Stretham records a century previously. The mill is situated in a wooded district, and its own grounds are thickly wooded. Woods Mill, as distinct from Wood's Mill. Or was it?

In the seventeenth century, Henry Wood Esq was churchwarden of Henfield. Not long after the turn of the century, in 1718, a week after purchasing the mill for £185, Richard Lish borrowed £200 from John Michener, yeoman, of Steyning. Repayment was to be made in instalments and completed by 1722.

Soon after the agreement was signed, Michener died, and complications set in. The sole executor of his will, Richard Dendy, also died; not until several years later, when Dendy's widow re-married, was any further attention given to the mill and the mortgage. In 1728, Richard Boreman of Steyning, gent., and Mary his wife (widow of Richard Dendy) resumed the case of the missing mortgage on behalf of the estate of John Michener.

The intriguing point about this transaction is that another lady stepped in. A lady from Henfield, Mary Wood, widow, paid the £200 to Mr Boreman. The Michener estate could be wound up, and Richard Lish was now in debt to Mary Wood. Had Henry Wood Esq been her husband or father-in-law? A churchwarden was a well-established resident; he coincided with that earlier mention of Wood's Mill; Mrs Wood obviously had a keen interest in it, to pay so much money. Those were the days when you could build a whole blind house in stone for under £20.

Richard Lish, having sorted the quick from the dead among his mortgagees, worked on until 1748; a capable miller would by then have had a goodly sum put by. He seems to have leased the property from Mary Wood, for when William Wood took over in that year it was on a lease and release arrangement. It was once more Wood's Mill, but Richard had made a good living and even acquired a little learning in his spare time. That last document is signed 'R.L.', in contrast to the cross on the first deed.

By the early nineteenth century Woods Mill had returned; Mr Wisden bought it from Mr Tippen, but was an absentee owner. Brighton lawyer wrote to remind him that the mill pond must be 'kept properly cleaned out' as a reservoir for the mill.

Through the next hundred years it changed hands several times, and milling did not stop altogether until 1927, but it was fortunate in its owners: the buildings were never derelict, and there was always a keen naturalist in possession, though one gentleman was a little disappointed: he used the waterwheel to generate his own electricity, but had to buy candles as well, for the water voles were so numerous that the banks of the stream were badly perforated, and the water supply was unreliable in the extreme.

Of all the caring owners, Dr J. Douglas Smith is particularly remembered; on his death, his family were reluctant to part with the property he had loved so much, so they presented it to the Sussex Trust for Nature Conservation. At that time (1966) the Trust had been established for only five years, and this generosity gave them the perfect nature reserve; in addition to the mill buildings, there are fifteen acres of land including marsh, streams, a lake and of course the woods. The waterwheel is in full working order thanks to a local expert. There are paths made of discarded millstones, and very attractive they are; some no doubt date from the days of a miller called Wood. The mill house has been turned into a dwelling for the resident warden, and also some lecture rooms, for the Trust uses Woods Mill as a college of natural history, to which parties of schoolchildren and students come regularly for day courses.

The mill itself is much as Richard Lish knew it. Those half floors needed firm support, and the brackets in position have served that purpose for two or three centuries at least. Whereas cruck beams were made from an entire tree-trunk or major branch, usually split into two, the mill brackets were cut from that angle formed where a branch curved out from the trunk of a

The Ancestors – but only by adoption

tree. The natural curve of the tree's growth has given the strength of steel through the centuries.

Out in the woods, among all the riches of natural history, lie the Ancestors – a nickname bestowed when their origins were uncertain. They are fragments of stonework, some being medieval figures, scattered in the undergrowth not far from the house, and creating a somewhat funereal atmosphere.

After the First World War, the property was purchased by an eccentric and wealthy man from Brighton. Attracted by the idyllic nature of the woods and lakeside, he planned to build an elaborate mansion, but he began the project in reverse order to that followed by most people. He began by planning the garden, which was to be adorned by statuary, Italian style. He had no clear design; he simply attended sales all over the country. If he saw statuary, he bought it – old, modern, whatever the condition. All the purchases were left in the woods to await their ultimate disposition.

The mansion failed to materialize as the gentleman went bankrupt; the statuary, gently disintegrating through the last sixty years, lies where he left it. A photograph taken at half time – that is, about thirty years ago – shows several armoured figures lying in the grass. They are now somewhat reduced and damaged, but hardly of any importance to the mill's work as an educational centre and nature reserve. The Trust now has over forty nature reserves in Sussex, and Woods Mill is the administrative and exhibition headquarters. Two thousand years old, give or take the odd few centuries, and flourishing. Burgeoning, I should say.

Firle House, close to the great beacon, is another of the layered delights. It was started 500 years ago; the front which now graces the countryside is eighteenth-century.

In all that time, the house has been home only to the Gage family. They also graced the countryside, though on occasion their rank obliged them to undertake duties which must have seemed most uncongenial to gentlemen who were also gentle men. Well before they put down roots at Firle, there were Gages at Hastings with William. In the days of Mary Tudor, one of the family was Constable of the Tower of London; not the best period in which to be there, whatever one's function. Many years later another member of the family brought home cuttings of a delectable green plum from his travels in France, La Reine Claude, which was later renamed after him – Green Gage.

Sometimes this event is wrongly associated with the Gages of Firle, but it happened in the 1720s, and concerned Sir William Gage of Suffolk, whose connection with the Firle family had been forged by a series of mainly happy events.

Hengrave Hall, near Bury St Edmunds, was inherited by Lady Rivers from her own family. Her unhappy marriage ended in separation from Earl Rivers; one of her children was a most attractive daughter, Penelope. At the age of seventeen she had three suitors, and their anxiety led to a certain amount of irascibility. Lady Penelope threatened to banish them all unless they were more peaceable; then – surely meaning it as a joke –

she told them to be patient; she would marry them all in turn . . . one at a time, of course.

Many a true word is spoken in jest; it took time, but that joke became a fulfilled promise. The first bridegroom, Sir George Trenchard, very soon died. After a suitable interval, Sir John Gage of Firle married Penelope. They had nine children, and when he died in 1633 she needed several years to recover from the bereavement. Then she married that third suitor from so long ago, Sir William Hervey, who outlived her.

Hengrave Hall was inherited by Penelope's third son, Edward Gage, who was made a baronet by Charles II. Thus there was the ancient viscountcy at Firle and the new baronetcy at Hengrave, and it was the latter which in the late seventeenth and early eighteenth centuries boasted Sir William of botanical interests and the green plum. It is correctly known as the Green Gage, not the greengage.

Even so, Sir William was not the first to introduce the fruit to England. It was known here in the days of Lady Penelope, a century before Sir William, and it was then called Verdoch; this knowledge of it must have come from Italy, where it was known as *verdocchia*.

Verdocchia, from Italy; Reine Claude, from France; Green Gage, from Hengrave Hall in Suffolk; but not directly from Firle Place in Sussex.

Further north, at Leonardslee near Lower Beeding, there is a lake. Gardens spread from the house to the valley where woodlands are mirrored in a long, curving sheet of water. To create that, a tributary of the River Adur was dammed, hundreds of years ago; were it not so long, Capability Brown might have been suspected of a considerable share in the work. Twice a year the gardens are open to all; in springtime when azaleas, camellias and rhododendrons are in their full glory, and in the autumn, when the woodland makes its own glowing contribution.

The neat point about Leonardslee is that it is an old industrial site, a forsaken foundry. The lake was brought into being not for its beauty but as a power supply strong enough to activate great hammers weighing half a ton, heavy enough to deal with molten iron ore. That colourful and peaceful valley to which people escape to enjoy the brilliance of spring and autumn, echoed centuries ago to the noise of furnaces and forges, hammers and bellows, and the clank of the finished produce being carted away.

Had the old machinery been powered by coal, the area might now look like any other area of past heavy industry, with soot and slag heaps. Sussex has coal, but so placed that mining would be uneconomic. Timber was everywhere – vast forests stood ready for use. Wood and water left no residue apart from disused hammer ponds and thinner forests.

Wander around Leonardslee; enjoy its beauty. You are looking at a slag heap, Sussex style.

Highdown is modestly tucked away; from the A27, one could be too busy looking for Castle Goring; travellers on the A259 could be Worthing-bound and pass by, unknowing. A pity, to miss the only garden of its kind in the whole country.

It was made by a big-game hunter who turned his talents to flower-hunting; a steeplechase jockey who could adjust to the lesser speed of plants and trees; an army colonel, Military Cross, who still had an eye for rare plants whilst serving in the Sinai desert. This man of many talents also served briefly as an assistant private secretary to Lloyd George, but that was his last venture before turning entirely to Highdown; perhaps it was an encouragement.

Highdown Tower was by no means a stately home but it had, and still has, individuality. The tower rises among its surrounding trees, with a view straight out to the Channel. Built in the early nineteenth century, it promises solid comfort rather than any status symbol. It suited Frederick Claude Stern to perfection; the outdoor man *par excellence*.

The house stood on chalk downland, its only garden consisting of a couple of small lawns – one each side. Evergreen oaks protected it on the western side; beyond that, the ultimate in exotica, was an old chalkpit where pigs and chickens kept company with a rubbish tip. Their descendants might still have been there, except that the younger members of the household wanted a tennis court. The only flat ground on the small estate was the floor of the chalkpit, and 1909 was not the heyday of the mechanical digger, so the tennis court was made there. The existing décor – pigs, poultry and rubbish – was uncongenial.

The family decided to put them elsewhere, and to make a garden on the pit floor and also up its sides, which were in places at least thirty feet high.

With the decision made and the move accomplished, another problem loomed: what to plant. Many people, expert and otherwise, were swift with the answer: Nothing. No one could expect anything to grow on solid chalk. It never had, and never would.

They could have no garden in the usual sense, but the removal of the pigsty revealed an unsuspected lime kiln, giving rise to the idea of a water garden. They faced the kiln with Horsham stone to give the appearance of a cave, into which water ran from a pond which was dug out and cemented in front of it. Further away, still in the chalkpit, there was another patch where water collected during the winter; they cemented that too, and gave both ponds a light covering of top soil. At least they could try water lilies. The days of livestock and rubbish tip were over. The lilies flourished.

Between 1914 and 1918 'we all had other things to do' – but after that, the Chalk Garden came into its own, particularly after 1919, when Colonel Stern married another gardener; they devoted very nearly half a century to the work. As it progressed through the years, several books were written; the Colonel wrote, and the Colonel's lady was indispensable as proof-reader and adviser. Even when elderly, they worked together with the infectious joy of a couple of adventurous teenagers: 'January and February are a most exciting time of year . . . the common snowdrop is found all over Europe from northern Spain as far as Kiev . . . the finest form is the Warham variety which is said to have been brought back by soldiers from the Crimean war . . .'

Finding plants able to survive on chalk was not a problem for long; experts became friends, numerous friends were experts; expeditions went frequently, as in the past, to far countries in search of unusual plants and trees, and the Sterns were always ready to contribute towards the expenses, and to work on the seeds and cuttings sent back. Not that the travelling was always left to others: 'Rose Primula, one of the earliest bush roses, coming out at the end of April, becomes a mass of open single yellow flowers . . . on a hot summer evening it scents all the garden around. This rose came from the Arnold Arboretum near

Chalkpit Garden, Highdown – the impossible brought to life

Boston USA as a quite small plant which we brought back in a sponge bag in 1929 and is now (about 1960) about ten feet high. . . . it was discovered near Samarkand by F. N. Meyer in 1911.'

The Colonel had a specimen of the old-fashioned cabbage rose – red, and beautifully perfumed, said to have grown in Greek and Roman gardens. Two others were found, unnamed, in the garden of an ancient Elizabethan almshouse. They all flourished in the chalk garden. The Macartney rose dates from 1792, when Lord Macartney, having made a diplomatic and commercial visit to China, brought back a pure white climbing rose.

Geological maps were helpful. To mark lime areas, and then discover the indigenous plants and trees, was usually to find suitable material for the Sussex garden. Not Japan, nor much of North America; but China, Tibet, and around the Mediterranean; South America and New Zealand. The Colonel was also a talented scientist, and in his laboratory his researches provided much information on improved methods of horticulture. He was becoming famous, and Highdown was rarely without some fellow enthusiasts in the guests' rooms.

Kew Gardens had received seed of a little yellow rose from Persia, and they entrusted some to the Colonel, who sheltered his seedlings in a greenhouse. All went well until a 1942 bomb shattered the glass; still the little plants grew, untroubled by the great winter of 1947. They had second thoughts after a second bitter season eight years later; then the Sterns read about the Persians using such bushes as firewood. Nothing venture . . . the Highdown fireplaces used rosewood for a brief period, and the Persian bushes, so severely cut back, flowered as never before. It was during that same period that the Colonel and his lady became Sir Frederick and Lady Stern, an honour bestowed for services to horticulture.

They worked with the long-term view so typical of gardeners: '*Osmanthus delavayi* is a first-class plant when covered with white flowers. It does not seem to be long-lived; one of our plants after about twenty years began to go back and died . . .'

A huge vocabulary of botanical terms was used with the ease of a native language, but sometimes laced with a sense of humour. The name of one evergreen bush proved too much even for the joint memories of Sir Frederick and his wife: '. . . *Fatshedera lizei* . . . a bigeneric hybrid, a cross between *Fatsia (Aralia) japonica* and an ivy, *Hedera hibernica*, made by a French nurseryman, Messrs. Lizé Frères of Nantes. Some of us can never remember its name, so it is known in the garden as "Fatheaded Lizzie".'

No wonder. The variety of plants in that garden was so tremendous that it was a botanical United Nations.

The Sterns' great friend, Mr Bowles, had a similar garden, though not cultivated on chalk; he found, as they did, that some plants were contrary, behaving against all the usual rules of their own species – blooming at an unusual time of year or producing flowers or seeds of unexpected colours and shapes. Those crazy curios were gathered together by Mr Bowles into a reserved section, known as his lunatic asylum.

Sir Frederick had no lunatic asylum for his plants, but one seems to have been particularly crazy: *Galanthus corcyrensis* – to ordinary folk, a snowdrop – but what an extraordinary snowdrop. It originated in Corfu and Sicily and had a very strange timetable: '. . . in full flower, and delightful; it is a wonderfully punctual plant, always coming out on 10 November or thereabouts whatever the weather . . . after a severe night's frost, which we often get at the end of November, the stems lie flat on the ground; then as the milder weather comes, up they get again looking as fresh as ever.'

There was a crazy crocus too, *Crocus laevigatus* by name; it flowered in November and through December, though not keeping to any special date like the snowdrop.

Quite early in the Chalk Garden's development, a knowledgeable friend had suggested peonies – 'paeonies', as Sir Frederick preferred to call them. They flourished – indeed, they flourished on that chalk as well as anywhere else in the world, and the Sterns became acknowledged experts. One strain grown at Highdown was named Sybil Stern, after Lady Stern; a tree paeony with velvety, rich red crinkly petals standing out against the softly green foliage. Varieties came from widespread sources: the Caucasus, Persia, China, Kashmir, France, Italy, Switzerland, Tibet; even Japan, usually the home of plants incompatible with Highdown soil, was able to send some.

One paeony was more widely travelled than many. It had been found in a garden in Kansu; a wild plant from the nearby mountains, it had been cultivated in the lamasery gardens. An American, Dr Rock, sent seed back to base, his base being the Arnold Arboretum in Boston. The Sterns received seedlings, noticing that the flowers, when they came, resembled some in a book on China – Kansu, in fact. When they wrote to Dr Rock, he replied that the lamasery and its gardens had been destroyed by bandits. The Sterns were able to send seed to help restore the garden.

In ancient Greece, Paion was the physician of the gods, and since ancient times paeonies were grown for their medicinal attributes. One type particularly caught Sir Frederick's attention, and he mapped the places of origin. It had been found on islands as well as the European mainland, from Cyprus to Steep Holme. Wherever it appeared, there had at some time been monasteries, to which people might look for medical treatment.

The Stern treatment for this difficult garden had been pretty constant from the beginning: it was generally considered advisable to plant three specimens of everything. One, where he thought it might grow; one, where friends thought it might grow; and another where no one thought it had a chance.

On that principle, and out of desperation, one of the first plants to be tried on the face of the chalk pit was St John's Wort.

An unduly large proportion of the next half century was spent in trying to get rid of it. To weed a near-vertical chalk face, up to thirty feet high, requires rather more than an afternoon with a gardening basket. An intrepid garden boy used to be let down on a rope, commando-style, to weed and to replant with more acceptable species.

Naturally there were failures, and disappointments other than St John's Wort. One was an elusive paeony: 'It miffs off . . .'

Even though their work was so widely recognized, Sir Frederick and his wife never lost sight of the simple joys of gardening. He would lean out of the bedroom window, savour the morning air of early spring, and gather a nosegay of April roses (but of course, at Highdown!) for her; tough little climbing roses pushing up high, even as far as the Tower roof. Yet they were not just a pretty bunch of flowers: they were *Rosa banksiae lutea*. Of course.

Sir Frederick died in 1967, and Lady Stern in 1972, yet people not fortunate enough to have known them personally may still make their acquaintance through the Chalk Garden. In all the years of its creation, the Sterns shared plants, seeds, knowledge and the great joy of their lives with all who cared to accept. At the end of their lives they bequeathed that garden of miracles to Worthing Corporation, to be open to everyone, a free gift from loving friends. It could not have been left in better hands, for the horticultural superintendent at that time had trained at Highdown.

Go. Even if your fingers are other than green, go to that garden of roses, paeonies, dianthus, Galanthus corcyrensis, great evergreen oaks, contented waterlilies, St John's pesky Wort, *et al*. Its makers are not there in person, but the growing things they coaxed into life are forever beautiful. We, most highly favoured, may go at leisure to enjoy the perfection they created from such unpromising land.

However, visitors must be content to depart at dusk, leaving the Chalk Garden shadowy and still – except, surely, for at least two fluttering moths.

1610 Speede map of Sussex

8 Name-Dropping

Early one morning, just as the sun is rising, get into your car and go. Make certain you have enough petrol to allow you to get lost, because that is your destination. A tour of Sussex fingerposts; names of tiny places, ridiculous and fascinating; brain-teasers, driving the reader into all sorts of intellectual acrobatics in the attempt to divine the correct meanings and derivations.

Take this as an appetizer: Great Wapses Farm. Roll it over your tongue; chuckle over the notion of Super Sussex Wasps revelling in some splendid orchard of plums – Great Wapses Farm. Make the most of it, for those lovely wapses began life as an Old English word for a pathway, and insects have no bearing on the matter at all.

Warninglid is pleasurable, but another snare. There is no lid and no warning, in spite of the vision of Saxon matrons clashing saucepan lids as anti-Viking alarms. Many names have passed through the melting-pot of time, and the Old English have been there so long that like the characters in a book, they bear no relationship whatever to living persons etc. This one is merely the name of a man who owned a small piece of land; if you have an ounce of romance tucked away behind that seatbelt, stay with me and the Saxon matrons.

All the names are not deceptive. Those beginning with Hart will have some connection with deer: Hartwell, Hartfield. You may take Apuldram seriously; it does refer to an orchard, but the dram is more a matter of faith than hope. Thorney Island really did have an overdose of thornbushes long ago, though if one drives across it nowadays the thorniest encounter is with the military sentry who most courteously requests Madam to return the way she came. Boxgrove really was a grove of box trees, long before the abbey was built. Its trees may have flourished while the rich Roman and his slaves were coaxing the neat box hedges into their exquisite patterns at Fishbourne.

Windfallwood Common sounds a veritable *embarras de richesse*, not only an orchard for the windfalls, but an ordinary wood for the use of birds and badgers, and a common whereon the gentlemen may enjoy cricket, and the ladies may enjoy serving teas week after week ... after week. It used to be Winda's territory; he had no cricket, but doubtless his ladies were called upon to serve contemporary goodies such as broiled fish or spit-roasted hedgehog.

There are many Greens, often relating to our own time, more or less. Partridge Green, Cooper's Green, Potter's Green; White's Green and Hamper Green; Pound Green where, something over a hundred years ago, there would have been an enclosure for stray animals awaiting collection by their owners. Many villages still preserve the pound as an interesting historical relic – nothing to do with weights and measures.

If I refuse to seek further for any derivation, any rhyme or reason for the following, you will understand:

> Ginger's Green.

I have been there, but was careful not to ask about Ginger. Residents rarely know such things, and Ginger himself is so evocative that to relate him to some far distant, and now irrelevant roots would be churlish. This Green belongs to Ginger; long may it remain so.

Cackle Street, and Little Heaven; those who can read an orchestral score will know the expression 'Stet': meaning, 'let it stand'. These are as evocative as Ginger and his Green; they are above linguistic dissection. *Stet*.

Battle is triumphantly realistic; the site of one of the three battles central to British history before the twentieth century reaped its dreadful harvest: Hastings, Trafalgar and Waterloo. But what of Sweatings Lane, and Swanbourne Lake? A lake, fed by a stream or bourne, whereon swans grace the silence ... for Sweatings, read Sweetings.

> Lullay, my lyking,
> My dere son, my sweting ... Lovers' Lane.

I know about Glasseye Farm, and Peppering Eye Farm, but why gild lilies? *Stet*. Madamses Farm would seem to be a Sussex plural, just like those ghostesses on postesses.

Some names immediately recall the old days of Sussex iron: Cinder Hill, Furnace Wood, Forge Lane; Iron Brook, Minepit Wood, Huggett's Furnace –

> Master Huggett and his man John
> They did cast the first cannon.

They did, too. That was in the time of Henry VIII. And eventually the first Elizabeth was chagrined to find that the Sussex iron men were doing a roaring trade, selling their products across the Channel. In that trade they needed an inordinate amount of wood for the furnaces; that demand was drastically reducing the Sussex timber forests which were essential for shipbuilding to provide the navy which was essential for the protection of the south coast against the raiders from across the Channel . . . The Queen imposed numerous restrictions, but the furnaces did not cease to function for at least another two centuries. Meanwhile, the boys who dealt with the charcoal in some of those furnaces ended their working day with black faces immersed in quart pots at the inn of their local hamlet: Blackboys.

Tarring Neville – at first sight, sinister in its implications for Neville, except that that great family first owned the land at least seven centuries ago, and Teorra owned it in even more distant times; that explanation is permitted, if you will leave me to bask in the charms of Open Winkins and Brownbread Street. Foul Mile must surely be a reference to the famous state of Sussex roads, though Terrible Down seems to be an instance of folk memory; the hill where so terrible a battle was fought that blood flowed like a river in torrent. Poverty Bottom – a valley where the soil was too poor to provide a living; but what of The Denture?

This is a great curving bridleway, sweeping from the Roman road, Stane Street, to Fairmile Bottom just north-east of Arundel, and for most of the way passing along the edge of Houghton Forest. Such a name, on an Ordnance Survey map, is startling until one remembers the Sussex characteristic of condensed pronunciation, of which the classic example is Brighthelmstone which shrank to Brighton. Bearing that in mind, and also the route of the bridleway, mostly edging along a forest adjacent to farmland, the mystery is solved.

There was, in the West Country, an ancient method of land-clearance and fertilization known as Devonshiring. It is uncertain just how ancient a method it was, but Walter Blith, an early agricultural writer, described it in his work of 1652, *The English Improver Improved*. At that date, it must have been well established. Mattocks were used to clear the land of scrub, which was then burned, and the ashes dug back into the soil. Through the centuries the name shrank to Denshiring; in Sussex it shrank even further, into Denture. It was in frequent use – a necessary procedure in an area where the forest undergrowth needed to be kept under control, and clear of the adjacent farmland.

Returning to the charm department – what of Cross-in-Hand, and Three Cups Corner? One is said to have been a gathering point on the way to Rye, the port from which the chivalry of England set off for the Crusades. Three Cups Corner is further along the same route, perhaps where Mine Host would be privileged to refresh that dedicated company.

Peelings sounds mundane enough – the first thing that comes to mind is that it must be associated with a pig farm – but it is only a reference to an Old English tribe who once lived thereabouts. Carthagena Farm is better, a classic, once-and-for-all example of supreme make-do and mend. One of the galleons of the Spanish Armada foundered off Bracklesham Bay, and there is a tradition that its timbers were salvaged to build a farmhouse, a couple of miles inland at Somerley.

A Northiam cottage has a purposeful name – Farthings. Unusually, it has several wells in the garden, and at one time the owner allowed fellow villagers to fill their buckets at a farthing a time. But surely the most delightful name, the most conducive to day-dreaming, is Little Knight's Oast. Was there an oast-house? Perhaps a bequest to the knight's little son from a loving godparent? Little Knight's Oast: three words only, but the stuff of endless enchantment and infinitely pleasurable imaginings.

There is some duplication of place names – a thing to be expected in a large county. Offham occurs just north of Lewes and also near Arundel. East Dean and West Dean appear in West Sussex; East Dean and Westdean (note the subtle difference) appear in East Sussex. The pair in West Sussex are neatly placed, one each side of a small village called Charlton. East Sussex arranged things rather less neatly; Charleston Manor is not at all symmetrically placed, being just to the north of Westdean. No need for confusion; not if you sit very still and ponder carefully.

With Little London, proliferation is the word. The Chichester example has company in West Sussex, to the north between Easebourne and Graffham. In East Sussex Little London is near Heathfield, and there is another near Ardingley. Nothing could be better than to have Cackle Street twice over; once between Three Cups Corner and Netherfield, and also to the immediate north of Brede, upwards from Hastings on the map. Friday Street comes near Horsham and also to the north of Eastbourne.

Near-duplication causes confusion. Walberton is in West Sussex, south of the A27 between Chichester and Arundel, but Walderton is not too far away – further west, north of Bosham and Funtington. For good measure, Warbleton is on the other side, tucked away to the south-east of Heathfield.

Ifield, almost small enough to lose, comes between Horsham and Gatwick; Isfield, between Lewes and Uckfield, is no teeming metropolis. If you cross the A27 south of Lewes, taking the little road to Southease, Iford awaits you. Stand not upon the order of your going; continue southwards a mile or two further, crossing the river at Southease, and you will be within sight of Itford Farm, standing at the foot of Itford Hill.

Nicknames tend to be repeated. The Church in a Wood applies to at least two small buildings; one near Hastings, where it is associated with an old love-story of which there are several versions, about a young couple who plighted their troth on a cliffside seat nearby. Another is St Bartholomew's, near Cross-in-Hand. It dates only from the mid-nineteenth century, built to serve a private estate, and is now almost alone, hidden among trees. It has no churchyard, but there is an unusual memorial against the outside wall: a hawthorn bush. The founder of the church had been happily married to a lady whose maiden name was Thorn, and the bush has been a modest but thriving memorial to her for over a century.

The title 'Cathedral of the Downs' has at least three claimants, not surprisingly, there being a lot of Downs: the great church of St Peter at Treyford, which lasted so short a time in a material sense, yet somehow lives on in spirit; Alfriston church, so much more impressive than the little churches of the surrounding

The Church in a Wood, with its memorial to a happy wife

villages; and perhaps the most deserving of all – Lancing College chapel, the brainchild of an impecunious curate with a combined genius for educational vision, organization, fund-raising, and finding the right people to carry out his ideas. His architect designed a chapel described as the finest piece of pure Gothic put up in England since the Reformation. It is a mere century old, more or less, still incomplete in some respects but a cathedral in appearance and conception. Above all others, the Cathedral of the Downs.

Some names are strangely coupled. Of Upper and Lower Beeding, the former is, as it were, down south, on the low ground through which the Adur flows near Bramber. Lower Beeding is up north – at least twenty miles away by road and on much higher ground past Leonardslee and Warninglid. Bognor Regis was merely Bognor until 1929 when King George V convalesced there. It had, in early times, been a Saxon settlement. Little Bognor is about eighteen miles inland, northwards of Littlehampton; it is said to have been a grazing pasture for the pigs belonging to the Saxons of the coastal settlement at Bognor. Unless the slaughtering was done *in situ*, the bacon must have been very lean, to say nothing of the swineherd.

Not only swine went walkabout. Sometime between the sixteenth and seventeenth centuries and our own time, Eastbourne did that very thing. John Speede knew such a place and marked it on his 1610 map; it was deep into West Sussex, on a bend in the River Ems just north of Thorney Island. He also marked Ebourne in East Sussex, but it was well inland from 'Pemsey Haven'. In the 1770s, Gilbert White knew East Bourn, but by the nineteenth century it was East Bourne. Nowadays, Speede's Eastbourne has become Westbourne; Ebourn has become East Bourne, still in its old position and preserved as the Old Town, but it has also taken to the beaches and turned itself into Eastbourne.

Before it changes its mind again, leave Eastbourne; leave it and Pevensey behind you. Keep going eastwards along the A259, and you will pass, on your right, Barnhorn Manor. Keep going, still eastwards; about half a mile further along you will pass, also on your right, Barnhorn*e* Manor. Intriguing . . .

After that, you may care to look at a few public houses. They rarely have the bouquet of ancient place names, but there are some of more significance than the conventional hostelry names. The Angel, at Midhurst, is the subject of a very likely story; it is one of the inns at which the Pilgrim Fathers paused on their way to embarkation for the New World. They are said to have renamed each such inn 'The Angel'; one assumes that the reception was uniformly kind. They were setting out on an adventure such as many people of their day (early Stuart) longed to undertake; their sober attire did not affect the aura of glamour which borrowed something from the dashing memories of Drake and Raleigh and from the valiant endurance of martyrs less than a century before.

At Cocking, the Richard Cobden Inn commemorates the local man who worked selflessly for free trade in the mid-nineteenth century. So intently did he work that his own affairs came near to bankruptcy, but he was saved by an extraordinarily generous public subscription. Dunford House was built on the site of the farmhouse where he was born, and he spent his last years very comfortably there. It is still in use as a conference centre, with most of his treasured possessions in place; a beautiful, serene retreat in which concentration comes easily.

The Snowdrop Inn has sad connotations, but the Chalk Pit Inn is not far distant. It is to the north of Lewes on the A275. There is no connection with the garden at Highdown; here, the chalk-pit was used as such – a good source of income. The problem of haulage was solved ingeniously. Chalk, dug from a pit behind the inn, had to be taken to barges on the river the other side of the road. The gradient was steep. Two brick-lined tunnels were constructed beneath the main road, with tracks on which chalk-filled trucks could run down the steep incline to the waiting barges below. It was known as the Offham Tramway; in essence, a miniature railway, and one of the very first in this part of the country, constructed in 1807.

To control such heavy freight on the slope, the trucks were held by a cable passed round a wheel at the top. Even so, the presiding engineer, William Jessup, felt that an extra safeguard was desirable, and he designed a propellor to be fitted on each truck at right angles to the travelling direction, something like the modern use of a parachute as a brake. Advanced thinking indeed.

An alternative mode of transport comes to mind with the name of the hamlet Gotham, a couple of miles inland, to the north-west of Bexhill. Maybe, in the days of its three wise men (those of the nursery rhyme, not of Bethlehem) it was nearer to the sea, like Pevensey Castle.

> Three wise men of Gotham
> Went to sea in a bowl.
> If the bowl had been stronger
> My story would have been longer.

Talking of nursery matters, in the north-west of the county, near Elsted, there is a clutch of names almost within walking distance of each other: Turkey Island, Goose Green, Foxcombe Farm, Trotton and Nyewood. What could be more apt, for readers of Beatrix Potter? She might also have been associated with Shufflesheeps, but that is a dozen miles away from this little group, just south of the Surrey border.

There are sundry solemn and expert explanations for Bopeep Farm near Alciston; but for a farm in sheep country, at the foot of Bostal Hill which has a dew pond at the summit, surely Bopeep was a natural choice?

Jack and Jill went up the hill . . .

The Jack and Jill public house in Clayton also takes us into the nursery world; Jack and Jill really did go up Clayton Hill. They are the two famous windmills of which Jill arrived first. She was built in Brighton, just after the Prince Regent had at last become King. Not until thirty years had passed was she moved to the top of Clayton Hill; all complete, just as she was, and drawn by over eighty oxen. That Jill was a post mill made the task slightly less difficult than it sounds; she had only to be detached from a central pivot. In 1876 Jack, a tower mill, was built nearby. Black Jack, White Jill; they worked until well after the turn of the century, and into their old age.

> Jack fell down
> And broke his crown –

Not really. A flash of lightning did it for him, and he stood for many years with ruined sails. In the 1970s a film company needed the mills as part of a set for a big production, and they were restored to their original appearance, just as strong a reminder of Sussex as all those lesser-known names of tiny hamlets and ancient streets.

Bodle Street Green; Little Twitten; Riders Bolt; Pondtail Copse; Hellingly Horselunges; Five Lords' Burgh; Knockhundred Row . . . when the outside world becomes stressful, find a place alone, even if only by closing your eyes. Think back to olden days when people carried nosegays to ward off the plague. What else is stress, but a modern plague? Gather nosegays of these lovely, evocative names and let them waft through your mind. Wildham Wood; Highnoons Farm; Sparks; Sweet Willow

Shaw; Sherwood Rough; Didling; Hundredsteddle; Beggars Barn Shaw . . . savour them. The peace of the Sussex countryside is more tranquillizing than any pharmaceutical remedy.

Last of all, there is a most special name. A name fit to be set upon a velvet cushion at the pale feet of the Muses, for its owner expressed joy and reverence and compassion; most of all, he expressed devotion to the county of his birth.

Charles Dalmon.

Yes? But if you say No, you are in company with many local experts. Many people born and brought up in Sussex look blank when they hear the name; yet few counties can boast so devoted and talented a poet. Sussex haunted him, heart and soul; he was imbued with its atmosphere and its beauty – it was the central theme of most of his work.

> Men scarcely saw him as he passed along
> And few were they who listened to his song;
> He laboured with the lowliest, and gave
> His love to Sussex till he reached his grave.

He was not one of those very parochial Sussex men who felt that to venture more than ten miles from their native village would be to brave the chill winds of foreign parts. His work reflects beauty from the whole wide county – no mean achievement for a working man in pre-car days. He was the son of a coachman, born in about 1862 in Old Shoreham, and descended from William Damon, lutenist to the first Elizabeth. His first love was Sussex, his second love was the poetry of Shelley, and his overpowering love was the making of his own Sussex poetry.

To a Skylark Singing on a Meadow Gate near Chanctonbury

> My little friend, have you assailed
> The shining gates of Heaven, but failed
> To gain admittance there, and so
> Return to kindlier ones below?

Dalmon won the friendship and admiration of Edward Thomas, the younger and greater poet who was killed in France in 1916. Presumably for working reasons, part of Dalmon's life was spent in London. It was exile, but Edward Thomas wrote: 'Before Mr Belloc and Mr Kipling, Mr Dalmon was a Sussex poet ... even in Chiswick he knew a dryad. She haunted a mulberry tree in an old garden ...' As if underlining that, Dalmon wrote:

> Oysters make pearls
> Of alien things ...

The fact was, that he was never really torn away; the bond was unbreakable, and he carried its beauty forever with him. Here is that Crawley weathervane, soaring from the top of its steeple.

> Vainly to churls the gentle poet sings,
> But no wild flood can rise
> To drown the dove that flies.

He was the flying dove, the gentle poet, and neglect often depressed him. Yet the thought of Sussex legends and customs, specially in conjunction with the poets' panacea, springtime, brought the joy bubbling back again. Heathfield's Cuckoo Day, for instance. The old woman of legend came to Heathfield Fair in April, carrying a basket; she opened it, and out flew the first cuckoo. All glory was let loose, borne by the golden-hooved sun horses.

> ... where the sun-horses chafe in the sun-god's hold
> Just over the eastern downs;
> Till the flash of their bits and their harness-chains
> And the lightnings tied into their tails and manes
> Shoot over the Wealden towns,
> Shoot on to the Cowfold monast'ry spire
> Shoot out to the sweeps of Chiltington Mill
> To Tennyson's windows on Blackdown Hill
> And the sky of the neighbouring shire.

Note the reference to Tennyson, who had personally comforted Dalmon in a moment of depression: 'How can there be failure, if the divine speak through the human, be it through the voice of prince or peasant?'

There were several small volumes of poetry, one dedicated to Chanctonbury 'with the love of a lifetime'.

Dew on the Downs

When we are fast asleep
Do pitying angels fly
Low down the sky
And weep?

For they must see, each day
How, for the devil's toys
We throw God's joys
Away –

Must see, from Heaven above
How we, in lust and greed
Pay little heed
To Love,

And through our lives forgo
All that would bring more
   near
God's kingdom here
Below.

This knowing, hid from sight
While we are fast asleep
They may so weep
All night,

That when the dawn appears,
Trees, flowers and grass are set
All glistening wet
With tears.

His thoughts were not entirely of the countryside; there were some raw moments, as when a baby died, and again when Edward Thomas was killed:

> O, I could weep for bygone years!
> But memories grow too sweet for tears;
> And that which was can never end
> While memories last, my gentle friend.

How Dalmon managed to afford a journey to Provence is difficult to imagine, but even there, enchanted by the new experience, Sussex still obsessed him:

> I heard Ben Jonson's 'Drink to Me Only' sung
> At a Provençal dance,
> When the full moon paused, and hung
> Low over France.
> Where fireflies sparkled in the air
> Between the vines,
> And red pomegranate blossoms seemed to share
> The sunset hues of rosy wines.
>
> The song was sweet with all that I had known
> When I was still a lad,
> And left me all alone
> Home-sick and sad:
> I was a stranger in a land
> Of alien mirth,
> Thinking how beautiful the white cliffs stand
> Along the loveliest shore on earth.

Loving Sussex so much, he longed for his poetry to survive; they were interwoven, his poetry and his countryside, but there was always an aching doubt. The last plea is poignant:

A Voice from a Grave

> Ears of that footfall above ground pray listen to me!
> Are you a young man, a singer, with love in your face?
> A young man, a singer, with pity and love in your face?
> I have waited, and wearied for you, if at last you are here.
>
> What singers are now in the world, and what songs do they sing?
> Do they know that I sang, do they keep any song that was mine?

Do they care that I sang, do they love any song that was
 mine?
*Tell me, young man, young singer, did I sing one immortal
 thing?*

[Dalmon's italics.]

Find out for yourself. Those five slender, shabby books have been half a century out of print. One main reference library has an incomplete set; another has one solitary little volume overshadowed by thicker, newer books with visible titles on their spines. Charles Dalmon's works are very easy to miss, but they stand waiting; the beauty and inspiration of the Sussex countryside glow within those neglected pages. Open them, and you will see it all through his eyes.

*Tell me, young man, young singer, did I sing
one immortal thing?*

Yes, indeed.

9 Glory, Alleluia

When the middle days of March are edging into springtime, those wonderful Downs are still visible from below through a tracery of tiny branches; sometimes, specially in the early morning, they are hidden by heavy mists enfolding the summits.

Ask someone to drive you; perhaps westward, out of Lewes, while the first sunlight reaches across the surface of lower slopes and lesser hills, lifting a froth of white vapour so that it hovers, glittering above the grass in a drift of swansdown.

Trailing Mists

Nor book nor toy nor jewel seems
To please the lady of my dreams —
Oh, if I could but take to her
These veils of glistening gossamer!

Charles Dalmon found this enchantment in the Cuckmere Valley; I suspect that every lover of Sussex has a favourite place in which the glory is all-enveloping; full of blessing and peace.

How else to attain peace?

Once upon a time, in Baghdad, there was born to an Arab named Abdullah a son, also named Abdullah. The family combined that nationality with the Jewish faith; they possessed vast wealth.

By the time the son inherited, he had developed anglophilia to such an extent that he sought an abode in England and purchased a mansion in Brighton, only a few yards from the sea. He changed his name to Albert, having become a close friend of Prince Albert's eldest son, who was at that time still Albert Edward, Prince of Wales. Though the latter did not become King Edward VII until after his friend's death, they were such kindred spirits that Abdullah/Albert would more correctly be considered an Edwardian rather than a Victorian.

Being thus far anglicized, even to the point of acquiring a baronetcy, he nevertheless retained his Arabian ancestors' fatalistic attitude to death. A thoroughgoing Edwardian would have made provision in his will, delegating to his executors the task of erecting a lavish mausoleum in some fashionable necropolis. But Albert Sassoon's Arabian blood was far from dormant. His body must rest in splendour when the spirit had vacated it, just like those of his English friends. He ordered a splendid Oriental mausoleum, almost as full of Eastern promise as the Royal Pavilion – indeed, there was a strong resemblance. Not only that, but the thrifty-Jewish, fatalistic-Arabian, splendour-loving Edwardian intended to get his money's worth before as well as after. The mausoleum was erected right next door to his mansion, from which the splendour was in full view; a home from home, as it were, but not too far from home. All of six feet away.

In 1896 Sir Albert Sassoon died, and took up residence next door to his old mansion; however, he had not taken into account, in planning for eternity, that descendants might not approve his taste. He had been a lovable character, and it seemed unfitting that he should take his final rest at the very roadside – almost on the footpath – of a very busy main road; a corner site to boot, where the noise, even of horsedrawn traffic, must be at its very worst. The family endured such a situation as long as humanly possible, but by 1933 the horses had given way to motors; Sir Albert was removed and re-interred more suitably in London. His ex-mausoleum became a decorator's store. During the Second World War, it was used as an air-raid shelter – the Victorian builders had wrought sturdily for their £6,000. Now it belongs to a local brewery, who in 1953 opened it as an annexe to their adjacent public house. The interior of the Bombay Bar was carefully redecorated and furnished, in keeping with the Oriental style of the exterior – houris, elephants *et al.*

Soon, the building will have served as long, and longer, in that capacity than it originally served as a mausoleum, not to mention its very useful interim roles. Sir Albert would probably have felt it was worthwhile after all.

In the year when Sir Albert's tomb underwent its most startling metamorphosis, 1953, battle royal was being waged in Arundel over the fate of another building, the Maison Dieu. Its sturdy ruins stand on the river bank between the castle gate and the bridge, and it was founded by an Earl of Arundel, Richard Fitzalan. An almshouse to accommodate twenty poor men, it was gently monastic; the sort of foundation which great men would bestow in compassion, and lesser men gave with an eye to their own eternal welfare. In 1396 Richard saw it completed; what his feelings might have been in 1397 as he knelt before the headsman must remain uncertain, but his little Maison Dieu continued its good work until it met its own executioner, in the guise of Henry Tudor's destruction of all things monastic. Perhaps it was poetic justice (depending upon one's taste in poetry) that Henry regarded the current Earl of Arundel favourably and returned to him the lands and buildings which his unfortunate predecessor had bestowed upon Maison Dieu. When, a century later, the Roundheads attacked the castle, the smaller building provided good cover for their musketeers, though not without cost to itself.

It was a foretaste of the Sassoon mausoleum-cum-air-raid-shelter, but Maison Sir Albert was never threatened with the same lowly fate as Maison Dieu. Early in 1953 the local

Maison Dieu – a mildly monastic gift to Arundel

Authority were getting ideas, and a member of Arundel Town Council sent a clarion call to the local Press:

> ... It is to be hoped that they [the burgesses] will make it clear to members of the Council that the land on which in 1396 Earl Richard built the Hospital of the Holy Trinity to the Glory of God, and for the Relief of the Poor, is unsuitable for the erection of lavatories in 1953.

The Editor added a little note:

> The Council have since decided to seek another site ...

Pomp and circumstance: the Chichester Moon

As a result, the Relief of the Poor and any other interested parties is nowadays provided for in a small modern building on the other side of the road, while Maison Dieu remains, ruined but with unimpaired dignity, and a haggard beauty all its own.

Local dignitaries were not always flea-in-ear. The Mayor of Chichester, from the latter part of the seventeenth century, went splendidly forth after Sunday Evensong, upon his regular visit to the bishop. No coach, no sedan chair, no mettlesome mount; he went in solemn procession, attended by all the other dignitaries, walking in the light of the moon – even during high summer.

It was a very special moon, the Chichester Moon; about eight feet high, and a big strong fellow was needed to carry it before His Worship. It was a great spherical lantern on a long pole, nearly seven feet in circumference and over two feet deep, its curved panes made of transparent, topaz-coloured horn; inside, it had fittings for five candles, and it was surmounted by a gilt crown supported high over the upper vent. The Mighty may have come a slight cropper in Arundel, but in Chichester they rejoiced, even as late as 1962, when the Moon once again enjoyed, as it were, the limelight. It was carried in procession at the grand opening of the Chichester Festival Theatre, in the presence of many stars . . .

. . . and no doubt many kisses, and cries of 'Darling!' Some Sussex folk claim that handy institution, the kissing gate, as a Sussex speciality, though that is wide open to contradiction. It is ubiquitous – one of the more enchanting artefacts of the English countryside.

At the End of a Summer's Day

> I ask of fate
> No more than this;
> To find in our way
> A kissing gate,
> And claim one kiss.

The poet will forgive me for forgetting his name since I so well remember his poem. Doubtless there is someone else, somewhere, who also remembers it.

Strangely silent – the kissing gate at Clapham church

These little gates are often to be found; one gate, only one gatepost; where the opposite gatepost would normally stand, a U-shaped fence curls around so that only one person at a time may pass, and that at very reduced speed. Our poet thought he knew the purpose and so, indeed, did I. However one must, albeit grudgingly, put forward another somewhat philistine interpretation which has been suggested:

These gates are said to close with a slight, very slight swishing sound; a very slight kissing sound – that is why they are known as kissing gates. So it is said.

Clapham church is in as romantic a spot as one could wish. A narrow path leads upwards through the woods and into a clearing veiled by the branches of a great tree on the green. The old church stands to one side; its grounds are entered either through the lychgate or the adjacent kissing gate.

Try as I would, I could not persuade the kissing gate to produce that certain sound. In that lonely woodland glade, even the squirrels began to eye me strangely. It was not what they were accustomed to . . .

From the outside of a small church to the inside of a great

Grown old in service; a kissing gate in Clapham Woods

cathedral, the gift of the dukes of Norfolk to the Catholics of Sussex. The Cathedral of Our Lady and St Philip Howard; that was not its original dedication, in mid-nineteenth century, but it was re-dedicated in 1976 following the canonization of one of that great family. It stands high on the hill in Arundel, gracious and beautiful, blending with older surrounding buildings, without a trace of the raw newcomer.

Catholic churches great and small keep the major feast of Corpus Christi, but in Arundel it comes with a difference. Christ, entering Jerusalem, rode over palms thrown before him in spontaneous homage. At Arundel when the Host, Corpus Christi, is borne from the high altar down that long aisle between crowded worshippers, it is borne over a carpet of flowers. No hasty homage is here; all the flowers of early summer are gathered and worked into a carpet; indeed, at first sight it seems to be exactly that, but the colours of the floral pattern and the elusive perfume confirm that it is truly a carpet of flowers.

It is the climax of the celebration. The golden monstrance in which the Host is displayed is borne as the focal point of the procession; priests and their attendants move slowly along the carpet from the altar to the west doors, out and across the main road which is lined all the way by kneeling Catholics and equally reverent onlookers; on, through the crowds to the castle gates and into the courtyard for the final blessing. The scene is the ultimate in ecclesiastical splendour, but the carpet of flowers seems to outshine all else except the Host. The lilies of the field, time and again, eclipse Solomon in all his glory.

The cathedral of Arundel and the Howards has a floral carpet; St Paul's church at Elsted had Parkhouse's post office.

The incumbent, the Reverend Fernley E. Parkhouse was the inspired cleric who instigated a world-wide campaign, raising enough money to restore the tiny church which had almost been supplanted by the new one at Treyford. Though a past generation of parishioners had demonstrated their unwillingness to walk that steep mile when the old church – or what was left of it – was close at hand, a new difficulty had arisen with the advent of old-age pensions. Such benefits had to be obtained from post offices, but the nearest one to Elsted was in Midhurst; about four miles as the crow flew, but that mode of transport was not for pensioners. They had to go by the longer and more costly bus route.

The imperturbable priest gave the matter some thought, then he took a course of training. Elsted church had almost come into its own; Elsted rectory was about to follow suit. Necessary equipment was installed in one of the rooms: Fernley E. Parkhouse had become sub-postmaster of the parish, and Elsted rectory was probably the only one in the country to double as a sub-post office.

Government finance was not often in ecclesiastical vein; in Hastings for many years its main concern was to foil the activities of smugglers, who cheated the administration of much revenue.

At the foot of the cliffs, reaching to the water's edge and further at high tide, there used to be a great mass of boulders known as White Rock. It had been there for centuries, and there was no record of its advent, which had presumably been a slow development. In storms, waves were sometimes forty feet high – high enough to break over the top of White Rock, which through so many years had worn smooth. A road was cut across from west to east, but it was too often flooded. There was also a flagpole at the highest point, used by the excise men to signal to their colleagues waiting at a distance. They were exposed to vicious gales and violent seas, and their signals must have been as visible to the smugglers as to their colleagues.

So much flooding made the White Rock road too dangerous, and late in 1834 major alterations were put in hand. The Rock was demolished and the cliffs were cut back. The remnants were used as a basis for the present sea-front. During the excavation of the cliffs, ruins of a medieval chapel were found – St Michael's Chapel – which had once been on St Michael's Hill.

The disappearance of White Rock not only deprived the smugglers of some of their cover but gave the real tradesmen extra space. One of the first enterprises to set up was a brewery, catering for folk who could not aspire to smugglers' brandy. The coastguards, then known as the Preventive Service, moved themselves and their flagpole to the top of the cliffs, but there they had buildings, giving them some protection from the weather.

The site of the brewery later became the site of a building known as Palace Chambers, which was for many years the office of the Inland Revenue. Income tax officials, working to prevent tax evasion by twentieth-century smugglers and others, worked in comparative comfort, close to the place where former coastguards were at the mercy of winds, waves and murderous 'gentlemen'. Yet present-day excise officers have also to meet great dangers in dealing with arms and drug-smugglers, in places where safety is no prime object.

One might say that x, in the shape of Palace Chambers, marks the spot where ancient and modern meet: the Preventive Service, of small boats and brandy kegs, and Customs and Excise, of sniffer dogs, fast cars and helicopters.

Also in Hastings, another x, this time the police station, marks the successor to a previous police station which had four-star cells. That is to say, at least one four-star cell ... a cell so appreciated by its occupant that he said 'They treat me like a friend'.

It was in 1955, when the Hastings Christmas Chess Congress took place. The Scandinavian champion, at twenty years of age the youngest participant, arrived a day early, very late at night. His limited English, very limited cash and obvious weariness inspired the local police to memorable hospitality. Fridrik

Olafsson was made so very welcome, and found his cell so comfortable, that he went on to take joint first and second prizes with Korchnoi. A little different from his previous visit to Prague, when he was arrested in the street and imprisoned for a small error on his passport. The cell and the service, when compared to that in Hastings, left much to be desired. Chess would seem to be a more adventurous game than one might imagine.

It was fifty-fifty; Lindfield's hospitality, which enfolded C. B. Cochran on every visit he could recall since childhood, and his own love for so beautiful a village. Naturally the great showman appreciated an attractive décor, which was what Lindfield provided.

Strange, though – Sir Charles always claimed to be a native of Lindfield; *Who's Who*, and all other such compilations were told the same. 'Cocky' was a Lindfield man.

After his death in 1951, his family contradicted all that. The truth was that Sir Charles had been born in Brighton; to Lindfield he owed, not his origins, but countless pleasant memories. Which was indubitably the second very best of good reasons for making such a claim.

The same village gave poachers a different welcome. For many years the mantrap stood outside one of the shops; a huge contraption with fierce springs, like an elongated and reinforced rat-trap. In earlier days, it was concealed in the woods and could easily crush a leg or even a skull, depending upon the angle at which the poacher tripped across it. Now it is kept safely indoors; a most terrible curiosity.

Happy memories, horrific memories; Lindfield also provided an insight into medieval housekeeping. 'Barnlands', a fifteenth-century timber-framed house, had wearied somewhat beneath its weight of Horsham slabs, and it was given a well-earned overhaul. The workman discovered that the windows had been fitted with primitive draught-excluder: strips of oiled rabbit fur. So much for the conventional notion of the chilly medieval home, sliced by powerful draughts.

Two other timber-framed houses bear the name 'Anne of Cleves' House'. One is in Ditchling, and one in Southover High Street, Lewes. Both are beautiful buildings.

Barnlands; a medieval house with draught-proof windows

The Ditchling house is only a partial survival, an east wing having disappeared long since. It has a delightfully haphazard appearance, as though the builders worked only a little at a time as they felt inclined, with no prepared plan. Windows and chimneys, like afterthoughts, jut out in all directions; a staircase leads to the upper floor, but it is on the outside. Going to bed on a blustery night may have presented problems.

The Southover house is of very different character: patchwork, rather than haphazard, or a sampler, showing off every possible stitch in the builders' repertoire. Normal samplers came in silk or wool, in a rainbow of colours; this sampler house is worked in grey flint, tawny brick and tile, plaster which appears white against the other materials, and the speckled velvety texture of Horsham slabs which partly cover the roof timbers.

Two beautiful houses, both indubitably the property of the most fortunate of the six queens of Henry VIII, but she would never have been free to visit them. In 1540, from 6 January to 9 July she was Henry's queen, six terrifying months which ended with a visit from his emissaries. As they approached, she fell to the ground in a dead faint. They were there to dictate terms, and on one other occasion, so far, the King's terms had included axe

Anne of Cleves' houses at Ditchling and Lewes: consolation for a discarded queen

and block. This time, the terms were not ferocious – merely impertinent. The lady Anne, daughter of John, late duke of Cleveland, Guligh, Gelder and Barre, was granted denization (naturalization) subject to the condition that she did not leave England without licence – that is to say, that she asked Henry's permission if she wished to do anything other than stay put.

There were compensations. A vast amount of property was settled upon her. Apart from similar quantities in East Anglia and the West Country, the Sussex list was formidable. Even at the first count, nine Sussex manors, fourteen rectories, four farms, pensions (at the expense of Lewes and Michelham monasteries, lately dissolved), rents, tithes, lands, messuages – all as a reward for having relinquished that perilous throne; for losing the great privilege of being a wife to Henry Tudor. She had to be very careful; now that she was nominally English, nominally the King's sister, the slightest disobedience to His Majesty would rate as treason; the slightest deviation from the current devotional tightrope could be fatal. One of her own grooms, Maundevild, went to the stake on such a charge. Yet Anne, on the whole, could not help being happy in her freedom from that gross tyrant's constant presence; also she was free from her own family, who had knowingly put her into such danger.

And she was rich. Cleves had never been a wealthy country, but here the Lady Anne, the King's 'sister', wore a new dress every day – so it was said. Much that she owned, she would never see; it was essential to be close to the Court, able to pay grateful, lowly homage whenever required to do so; necessary to be under the all-seeing eyes with no chance of escape.

It was a better fate than many ladies of her birth could expect. Those two houses which bear her name may never have sheltered her, but their rents were part of the revenues which provided the few pleasures in her life: those heavily ornate gowns which gave English ladies the horrors; and the love of many poor folk. There were occasions when she must have murmured the German equivalent of Alleluia – but under her breath, for she could never be sure who was within earshot. That February morning in 1542 when her successor, the tiny and too appealing Catherine Howard, went to the block: Alleluia, to be so plain – but alive. To be virtually a prisoner, but not in the great grey Tower. Alleluia.

Meanwhile, the two beautiful houses in Ditchling and Southover, along with all the other properties, sheltered more fortunate folk, providing revenue to support their absentee landlady in the style to which she was compelled to become accustomed.

Royal housekeeping, absentee or otherwise, brings one directly to Brighton's Royal Pavilion.

29 October 1805, Mrs Creevey to Mr Creevey: 'Oh, this wicked Pavilion!... the Prince had got more wine than usual... he led all the party to the table where the maps lie, to see him shoot with an air-gun at a target placed at the end of the room. He did it very skilfully and wanted all the ladies to attempt it. The girls and I excused ourselves on account of our short sight; but Lady Downshire hit a fiddler in the dining room.'

It was hard on the fiddler, who seems to have been the most unfortunate of his calling. Mozart had from time to time been a fiddler in sundry palaces, and he was starved, frozen, snubbed and underpaid, but no one actually shot him. Anything was possible in the Royal Pavilion, that palace by the roadside which started life as a two-up two-down farmhouse. So the story goes, but like the fiddler, there is a hole in it.

In about 1780 George Augustus Frederick, Prince of Wales, developed several lumps on his neck. He had already noticed a tenderness when his valet tucked in the shaving towel, but when the swellings appeared he was alarmed, even though his physician diagnosed only glandular trouble. Sea bathing at Brighthelmstone would cure it.

Brighthelmstone? Was it fashionable enough? And sea bathing sounded very unattractive. He hid his lumps behind higher neckcloths. Out of sight, but not out of mind. The higher the neckcloth, the more starch it needed; the tender lumps were often raw. It seemed there was no choice.

Even then, the Prince might still have refused except that his uncle, the Duke of Cumberland, had taken a house there; some sort of social life must exist. Sea bathing would be horrid, but it just might work, and there was nothing to prevent one's taking a glass of brandy after the compulsory drink of sea water; what was more, a visit to Uncle Cumberland would be sure to annoy the King. It was settled.

The Prince was pleasantly surprised. The place was called Brighton now, and it was quite civilized. All ranks turned out to welcome him; the church bells rang, the guns boomed, and Grove House was a very comfortable mansion. Even the chilly bathing was worth the effort. Ladies were immersed by female dippers; gentlemen were dunked by bathers, of whom the most popular by far was Smoaker Miles; the Prince found him to be an entertainment in himself. The same could not be said of Uncle Cumberland.

When the bathing season re-opened the following year, the Prince was anxious to return; Grove House was to let, minus Cumberland; also the following year. Then, someone with more capital than the Prince purchased it outright.

At that time the Prince was in dire financial straits; his vast debts and expenditure compelled him to close Carlton House, his London home. Neither Parliament nor his father would help him, and he could not afford to buy another house. A strange situation, for a Prince of Wales. Weltje was sent to Brighton in search of a house to rent.

Louis Weltje was the Prince's chef and general factotum, uncommonly ugly and an inveterate moonlighter. He needed to be, for his salary as royal chef was about as reliable as the weather. His eye for sale-room bargains brought a considerable income; later, he turned also to money-lending. He already had considerable reserves from his younger days as proprietor of the Coconut Club, near Brooks's, in London. Now, his searches took him to the property next door to Grove House; Brighton House. It was a very different abode.

Contemporary descriptions are largely in agreement. It was a neat, respectable farmhouse, two-storeyed, double-fronted with twin bow windows. Alternatively, it was a pretty cottage in a small piece of ground where a few shrubs and roses shut out the road, and the eye looked undisturbed over the ocean. It was offered furnished, at an annual rent of £150, with option to purchase at the sum of £3,000. The Prince could hardly afford 3,000 shillings, but Weltje took up the tenancy and sublet the house to his master.

Which is where we pause for thought.

The Royal Pavilion – Brighton's best council house, under repair

Two up, two down. Presumably there were service rooms also, tucked away somewhere at the back of the building, but the owner's accommodation was simply the four rooms, built on that small piece of ground. And the asking price was £3,000; alternatively the annual rent, £150; in 1786.

Nearly two centuries later, in 1965, it was still possible to buy an attractive four-up, five-down cottage of the same vintage as Brighton House, in its own small grounds, for less than £5,000. I know, because I did, and that memory sent me back to the newspapers of the 1780s, and their advertisements.

The *Bath Chronicle and Weekly Gazette* recorded events and sales in and around another upper-class watering place. Vendors were secretive about their asking prices but clearly stated their current rents, presumably because purchasers most often bought properties as investments, adding the rents to their income. Thickwood Farm offered 114 acres of freehold arable, meadow and pastureland with a good stone house, barns, stables and other requisite appurtenances at a yearly rent of £70.

Alternatively one might choose 'a valuable and desirable freehold estate consisting of a farmhouse, barns, stabling and convenient offices together with 153 acres of rich arable and pasture land, and 30 acres of coppice wood – be the same a little more or less – all inclosed and tythe free except the tythe of hay; also two cottages. The whole let to Mr Ballard at £160 per annum.'

But Brighton House, two up, two down, on so small a site, shielded from the road by only a few bushes – £150 a year.

A curiosity indeed. Perhaps by that time it profited a little by reflected glory from Grove House next door, lately bought by the Duke of Marlborough. At first sight, one wonders whether 'farmhouse' was a euphemism, like that farmhouse reputedly supplied with silver milking pails, where Marie Antoinette indulged in make-believe farming. Again, it was furnished; how, is not specified, but furniture for four rooms would hardly bring the property anywhere near to the value offered in the newspaper advertisements.

Any thought of sharp practice by Weltje may be discounted. He, more than anyone, was thoroughly aware of the Prince's financial embarrassments. To bite the hand that feeds you is stupid; to bite the hand which manifestly lacks the wherewithal is wasted effort.

The need for speed may have been an important factor. The Prince's London home, Carlton House, seen by everyone but himself as wildly extravagant, had to be closed, and he announced his intention of living as a private gentleman. That, as he saw it, meant living in penury and being ostentatious about it. To the rest of the world it meant that he was still thoroughly spoilt but had come nearer to brass tacks than anyone had ever thought possible. Actually the Prince was piqued, and showing off; his immediate needs were to impress his creditors and to be near Mrs Fitzherbert, whom he had secretly married.

On previous such missions Weltje had opted for a quick decision as though, if he had to be out of the kitchen, he preferred paintings to property. Possibly the owner of Brighton House saw him prowling and grasped the opportunity; Thomas Kemp was a member of that family who, among their other varied activities, were astute money-spinners via the building trade; the name lives on in Kemp Town, the district in which Sir Albert Sassoon chose to buy a mansion.

Therefore Weltje in his haste, combined with many other

pre-occupations, in one way did the Prince a favour by providing a house in which diplomatic impoverishment would be seen to best advantage, at a rent rather than a full purchase price; and a disservice in that both figures were somewhat oversize. He compensated slightly by agreeing that if the house were enlarged or improved, he would meet the cost and adjust the rent accordingly. It seemed an unlikely contingency.

The Prince moved in. He may or may not have noticed that the price of appearing poverty-stricken was high; he had never shirked paying for his pleasures. It was just that he expected Parliament to provide the money with which he paid.

It was said to be the happiest time of his life, and it lasted all of six months. So happy; how eminently logical, to enlarge that happy house. Enlarge the house, enlarge the happiness; the lease had been signed in October 1786, and by the following May the architect Henry Holland was sent for from Althorp in Northamptonshire to gild the lily at Brighton House. He built a replica of the farmhouse, and the twin dwellings were joined by a graceful circular drawing-room, a rotunda. Behind the rooms at the extreme ends of this new symmetrical building, service rooms were added, with a few essentials such as a coffee-room and a powder-room; to the northern block, a kitchen wing was also added, at an angle; beside the southern block lay Weltje's own house.

This was the Marine Pavilion. Here one sees that the aristocratic euphemism had indeed been in operation. A small piece of land, in that Capability Brown would have been hard put to find a vista or create even the smallest lake; there were no acres to spare for pasture or any of the other income-augmenting extras. But there was room for building, if carefully planned. The east front was practically on the roadside and always would be; the west front was a different matter entirely. Perhaps that was part of the fascination – the challenge of making a right royal appearance on a piece of land which would hardly have taken the stable blocks of any of the great country houses.

Henceforth those who had rejoiced in the Prince's simple life were well advised to absent themselves from Brighton unless in masochistic mood. The inhabitants rejoiced. To have the Prince of Wales as a short-term visitor season after season had been good for trade; to have him out of season, vegetating in a cottage, had been grim but mercifully brief. Yet in only three months that cottage was transformed into an imposing villa. It was like a gift from the gods. Its strange position, in full view of passers-by, was as good a commercial as any resort could wish, in addition to which the Prince and his lady were to be seen everywhere. Brighton was a boom town, thanks to Weltje's long stocking. He had paid out (so far) almost £22,500, and the Prince's rent had risen to a thousand.

Holland had decorated the Pavilion in the French style, cool, delicate, and elegant; but for centuries the Far East had beckoned, tempting the curious and adventurous. The Portuguese had long been on excellent terms with the Chinese; they founded trading and missionary settlements and brought back many examples of Chinese art which were much admired. Though *chinoiserie* never ousted Western taste, it was in great demand, offering as it did such a strong contrast. It was pictorial: springtime blossoms flowered perennially on wallpapers and vases; stylized trees stretched their branches to support fanciful birds; vivid dragons and serpents turned ancient symbols of shame and evil into fascinating exotica.

The Oriental tendency was not entirely aesthetic. One of the arbiters of the French style, Philippe, Duke of Orleans, had turned traitor during the Revolution, voting for the death of his cousin, the King. In Britain there was a wave of revulsion. The Chinese style was uncontaminated by treachery; what had been a fashion became a craze.

> In Xanadu did Kubla Khan
> A stately pleasure dome decree...

So wrote Coleridge, a few years after the Oriental transformation of the Marine Pavilion had commenced. Certainly no Englishman needed to travel further than Brighton, for the whole interior was newly decorated in the Chinese fashion. Oriental scenes enlivened the wallpapers; appropriate woods were used, and when unobtainable they were imitated. Plastic was well over a century away but the art of imitation and substitution was well advanced. A ceiling of rosewood and tea wood was planned for one of the salons; as they were unobtainable, they were convincingly imitated. Silk net hangings were

The Amaranthine Palace

common in China; in Brighton they looked identical, but they were made of wood. Bamboo was essential, and innumerable bamboo chairs went into the Pavilion – made from beechwood. A great staircase with balustrades of bamboo gave a light, airy appearance to the corridor; it was cast iron.

Sometimes East mingled with West; real bamboo would be combined with a common wood such as pine. Wallpapers were printed to look like bamboo trellis in different patterns; lights glowed within lotus-flower shades, held aloft by gilded dragons entwined around Spode porcelain.

It was startling. People had usually decorated one room 'in the Chinese taste' – but a whole establishment ... Lady Bessborough expressed a general opinion: 'In false taste, but for the kind of thing, as perfect as can be.' She was referring to the inside. The outside remained unaltered for much longer, though not for want of trying. Chinese designs were commissioned and rejected until, after years of trial and error, someone noticed that the Indian-style stables, built earlier, might very happily be imitated. At first, it was done with caution. Some of the windows in the main building were replaced by others of Indian style.

After that, there were great changes and the Pavilion became the Oriental fantasy we know today; the Royal Pavilion. Expansion was at the expense of Marlborough House, next door. First it was purchased and used as an extra wing of the Pavilion building. Eventually it was demolished, leaving space for further extensions.

Financially, the building was to be at Weltje's expense for twenty-one years. The main agreement between himself and the Prince in 1787 stipulated an annual rent of £1,000, rising to £1,500 after twenty-one years, but not even so astute a financier as his chef could keep up with the royal spendthrift. The rent was rarely paid, in spite of the incessant building costs. By 1793 Weltje was willing to sell the Pavilion to the Prince, the price to be decided by arbitration. £22,000 was a disappointing figure, but even that was not forthcoming. The nominal new owner was even able to raise a mortgage on what he had not yet paid for; Weltje had no Pavilion, no sale money, no mortgage. And — small wonder — he had left the royal service.

Fortunately money-lending is always a good standby; Weltje was a prosperous man when he died in 1800. Seven years later, his widow received repayment of the debt, and also an annual pension of £360.

It is interesting that the agreement on the purchase price was made at about the time when the Prince was being prodded into his official marriage to Caroline of Brunswick, when his debts were to be officially settled, and his emotions, at the mercy of so much officialdom, were torn asunder.

The actual repayment was made during his second honeymoon with Mrs Fitzherbert. Whether she directly influenced that action is uncertain, but the pension for Weltje's widow seems to bear her imprint. A sad imprint; the Catholic wife, as lawfully wedded as could be, set aside because she was Catholic; all for the sake of an official marriage to a German princess. For connoisseurs of irony, the sting in the tail of that story is that Caroline of Brunswick had been brought up without emphasis on any particular religion, so that she would be able to adopt the faith of whichever husband the future might bring her. She might well have spent her life as a Roman Catholic. As it happened, she was the Prince of Wales' Protestant wife, who had even less happiness than his Catholic wife . . .

The Royal Pavilion was also a sad thing, an architectural *Pagliacci*. Like Smoaker Miles, an entertainment in itself, though not so very entertaining for those who had to frequent it in those early days. An invitation was essential for people with any pretensions to social standing, yet once there, boredom threatened. Thomas Creevey and his wife were regular visitors, being close friends of the Prince and Mrs Fitzherbert. The social atmosphere there always bore a close relationship to the political situation elsewhere; when Thomas had to be away, his wife sent careful accounts of the latest events, some more dire than others. No crawler, she had offended His Royal Highness. After a few days, they met again: '. . . in return for a curtsey, perhaps rather more grave, more low and humble than usual (meaning – 'I beg your pardon, dear foolish, beautiful Prinny for making you take the pet') he put out his hand. We soon went to see the ball, and Mrs Fitz selected me to go in the first party in a way that set up the backs of various persons . . . We were soon tired of the amusement and sick of the heat and stink.'

Dancing could be compulsory, even when one's august partner had taken a drop overmuch: 'A waltz was played by the band, and the Prince offered to waltz with Miss Johnstone, but very quietly, and once round the table made him giddy, so of course it was proper for his partner to be giddy too; but he cruelly only thought of supporting himself, so she reclined on the Baron.'

Sometimes the polite world lost even the slightest veneer of propriety. All it needed was the presence of Richard Brinsley Sheridan, playwright, Member of Parliament, husband of a famous singer, and slapstick merchant extraordinary.

The Prince and some favoured guests were conversing in one of the salons; in came a local constable with a paper, supposedly a writ for the arrest of the Dowager Lady Sefton for playing illegal games of chance. It was Sheridan, exercising his stagecraft. Another incident occurred in a completely darkened room, where all the guests waited expectantly for a phantasmagoria (magic lantern show) to begin. Sheridan sat on a lady's lap. She happened to be a proud Russian aristocrat and failed to see the humour of his escapade.

For the last decade of his life the Prince was George IV, and when old age and failing health took their toll, he lost interest in the Pavilion. His brother, William IV, built extra guestrooms and used it as a holiday venue for family and friends, among whom was Mrs Fitzherbert, an old lady, much respected by her brother-in-law.

Queen Victoria did not need a palace by the roadside. The Isle of Wight offered the privacy needed by her young family, and much of the original Pavilion furniture was removed to other palaces. When the building was offered for sale, Brighton appointed a committee, and the purchase was agreed for £53,000. It had played so great a part in building the town's prosperity, and now it was to be the centre of its own conservation project.

Its originator would have been intrigued to know that it was the first important building to be lit by electric light bulbs.

Curious, that the other member of the royal family to take almost as much interest as the Prince was surely the most dissimilar in character: Queen Mary, the *grande dame par excellence*; her interest brought back much of the original furniture, and her advice helped to provide an authentic restoration.

Now the Royal Pavilion has surely come into its own: a museum, a concert hall, an educational centre; enjoyed and appreciated by thousands instead of the hundreds who formerly came to see and be seen. This Wicked Pavilion has come of age.

From the bulbous, gilded domes of Prinny's Pavilion turn westwards to the south of Arundel. In the grounds of Calceto Farm stand the ancient walls of tiny Pynham Priory. No more than twenty minutes' walk away, if one could go as in medieval days, stand the ruins of Tortington Priory. Between these two establishments Ellis Parker spent most of his life, and he was rather like Prinny: fond of the sound of his own voice, sure of the value of his own opinions, not over-sensitive about the feelings of other people, yet in spite of all that, somehow an attractive character.

He first came to the fore in 1478. Tortington Priory had been functioning quietly since the twelfth century; charity and worship, humility and devotion. Then came Ellis Parker, the sacrist. How long he had been there is not recorded, but on Relic Sunday in 1478 he erupted, and nothing was ever the same again. Not, that is, until they got rid of him.

Tortington Priory, the scene of Ellis Parker's unseemly protest

He must have been seething in silence for some considerable time, for no monk in his right mind would speak to the prior as Ellis did that day. When the relics of the saints – the most precious treasures of the priory – were placed upon the altar for worship, Ellis told Father Prior that it was idolatry, '. . . so causing unseemly dispute . . .'. No wonder. Monastic discipline was fearsome, and eventually Ellis had to apologize – the record says that he was duly penitent. It would.

News, bad or good according to the view of the beholder, travelled fast even in those days. The monks of Michelham were suffering disorganization; their prior was weak and full of years. They sent a petition: could Ellis Parker come as sub-prior?

He did, but not for long. Pynham, founded by the second queen of Henry I, was in a bad way. It was a tiny foundation with just a few men under monastic rule, whose work it was to keep the nearby causeway and wooden bridge in good repair and to give hospitality to poor travellers. It was just the simple, hardworking life to keep Ellis Parker's energy fully occupied. He was made Prior; not far from the place wherein he had

Moated Michelham: Ellis may well have assisted with the digging

sparked off unseemly dispute, but too busy to spark off any more.

Hastings had a bit of an unseemly dispute with a foreign warship in the seventeenth century. It is uncertain whether the ship was French or Dutch, but it bombarded the town, not so much with any intent to invade as merely to make things uncomfortable.

The oldest church, St Clement's, was hit by a cannonball. Tradition says that the ball embedded itself in the church tower; later reasoning suggests that so great an impact would have caused far more damage to the surrounding stonework and that the ball probably hit the tower and dropped into the churchyard. Whatever the facts, that ball is there is the tower now, as it has been for several centuries. At some time during the interim, possibly during a restoration in the late eighteenth century, some passionate devotee of symmetry fixed a second ball in the tower on the other side of the window; even then, they left the viewer in no doubt as to which ball was originally fired and which was placed there. Presumably, to deprive England's foes of any credit for such marksmanship.

Go to another ancient church, more ancient than St Clement's. Boxgrove Priory was founded at the beginning of the twelfth century by Robert de la Haye, and at the dissolution it was rescued from destruction by Earl de la Warr. There, you will find a grave inscribed: 'He died for England.'

The date is 17 August 1940. The young man's name was Billy Fiske, and he died at Tangmere, the aerodrome still preserved between Chichester and Arundel. In 1940 it was under fierce attack by the Luftwaffe, and Britain was short of men and planes.

On the morning of 16 August German planes attacked and the RAF counter-attacked. With the rest, Billy Fiske's Hurricane, P3359, took off, and they beat off the attack. His plane was badly damaged. At about one o'clock he limped back and crash-landed on the airfield. The plane burst into flames. The rescue team managed to get Billy out, and rushed him to hospital where he died next day.

So did many others, but Billy Fiske was unique. If you go to Tangmere, there is a roll of honour in the museum. There are nine names, nine members of the RAF in 1940, three of whom died in that year. They were all Americans. The USA did not enter the war until much later but these men came offering immediate help. At first there were just the nine. Swiftly the numbers grew; by 1941 they formed their own three Eagle squadrons. Billy Fiske was the first fatality, and he was buried at Boxgrove because it was connected with Earl de la Warr, an ancestor of the founder of Delaware State, which was where Pilot Officer Fiske had come from.

On Independence Day the following year, in St Paul's Cathedral, a bronze tablet was unveiled in his memory: 'An American Citizen, who died that England might live.'

He, and his friends. They could have stayed safely at home. They chose to come, and Billy Fiske is the symbol of them all.

How very curious: take one veteran to his old base, to the old officers' quarters, now preserved and turned into an absorbing

Tangmere: a veteran returns

museum; take him past the airfield where part of his war was spent, past the great hangars now put to good use as grain stores; but he goes direct to the old control tower – the only part of the whole complex which could use paint and putty and scrubbing brushes and any other handy restorative ... but one strongly suspects that it was left like that for sentimental reasons. Perhaps – judging from the veteran's expression – he thought so too.

Northiam had been sentimental about female monarchs ever since the magical visit of the first Elizabeth. She had feasted *al fresco* beneath the oak, eating the best that mine host of Hayes Hotel could supply. Queen Victoria never made a personal appearance, but communications were better, and villagers felt they knew her equally well. The Golden Jubilee, in 1887, was an occasion for real celebration; everyone contributed generously to the fund. A part of the land known as Hollow Fields was purchased from a local builder, Mr Perigoe, with an extra strip to make an approach road. Architects set to work, builders followed, and on 20 September of Jubilee Year the grand opening took place. It was a strange way to celebrate a jubilee, for what they had acquired was a brand new cemetery complete with two chapels. *Chacun à ses jollifications.*

In 1897 the Diamond Jubilee followed; the sum collected was smaller but by no means niggardly. This time they celebrated by buying a hearse. A do-it-yourself celebration hearse, made by Mr Kemp, a Hawkhurst craftsman, for £27.

It was a neat vehicle with a glass cover, designed not for pomp and ostentation but for the use of simple country people. If horse-power was needed, they had no waving plumes or glossy black steeds; the mourners gave notice to the farmer who owned the milk pony. Funeral days were overtime days for that animal. If that seemed too costly, the hearse could be pushed by hand. It was well cared for and fully insured against accident and fire; by 1919 the premium was £35, greater than the original cost. It was so well cared for that it was still in use until the 1939 war: 'Please supply:- pony for funeral Monday 19th October at 1 p.m.' (1938).

We all emerged from that war with changed ideas about our own dignity. Perhaps it was a great rebound after years of austerity; henceforth, hired limousines took us to and from our weddings and funerals; the matches and dispatches were almost equal in flamboyance. Northiam's little hearse would have seemed unbearably humble, even disrespectful. And yet that last sorrowful act, that final service, as when the disciples' feet were washed; surely it was far more meaningful than a whole cortège of gleaming cars.

There is no place better than Sussex for the stranger to put a foot wrong.

> You say eether
> But I say eyether –
> You say neether
> And I say neyether –

Yes, indeed. Remember Charles Goring, who planted Chanctonbury Ring and lived at Wiston? In fact he lived at Wisson. The Harmer family who made those cherubic memorial plaques hailed from Heathfield, and their house, somewhat glamorized and enlarged to suit twentieth-century taste, is there to prove it; but no: they lived in Heffle.

How William of Normandy pronounced Pevensey is a moot

point, but I doubt whether he got it right according to the locals: Pemsey. Who could possibly guess that Selmeston is really Simson? Or that Lullington is Linglen? Should you search for little Ifield which was previously mentioned, you may not find it unless you ask for Ivel. Hyffold is Eyefold; Hartfield very pleasurably becomes Hartful. Whatever Mary Delorme may have told you, Ellis Parker did not provoke his unseemly dispute at Tortington, but at Torton.

It is intriguing to compare the names on signposts with the names one hears; then to compare both with the names written on an old map, such as John Speede's Sussex map of 1610. Pevensey is the written direction; Pemsey one generally hears; on the old map, the Rape is Pevensey but the haven and the town are Pemsey. Hove is on the signposts and modern maps; long-term residents may be heard to say Hoove, and it is Hoove on Speede's map. Signposts say Steyning; residents all very firmly say Stenning, and that is how Speede wrote it. We have Treyford on the signposts, but the locals and Speede say Trefford. Moulsecomb on modern maps is Mousecomb to Speede and the natives.

Folk memory clings sturdily, not only in such matters as the burial place of Canute's daughter; old names linger in ear and speech, while the written word changes through the centuries. One could probably explain this through the evolution of spelling; in the days of John Speede, a writer's ears made his spelling rules, and rules therefore varied from one writer to another; it was all flexible, which is partly why it is difficult, or amusing, depending on one's outlook, to read old manuscripts. Then the written word developed and standardized, acquiring a few complications in the process, but the spoken word tended to remain faithful to the older ways.

In this, as in all else, generalization is unwise. I was shepherding a stranger to the county, and she did some conscientious homework: for Bothiam, say Bodgem; for Bosham, Bozzum; for Udiam, Udgem; for Northiam, Norjam. Every (Sussex) schoolboy knows.

And she spoke to a long-time resident of that village; an acknowledged expert. Tentatively, she asked, 'Norjam – I hope my pronunciation is correct?'

'Actually, I say Northiam . . .'

Farewell.

Bibliography

A History of Sussex, J. R. Armstrong (Phillimore, 1974)
Sussex, John Burke (Batsford, 1974)
A Guide to Sussex, John Cleland (Morland Publishing, 1985)
A View of Sussex, Ben Darby (Hale, 1975)
Lift Luck, Tickner Edwards (Methuen, 1931)
Castles in Sussex, John Guy (Phillimore, 1984)
Glyndebourne, Spike Hughes (David & Charles, 1981)
Dew Ponds: History, Observation and Experiment, Edward Martin (Werner Laurie, 1914)
The Place-Names of Sussex, A. Mawer and F. M. Stenton (ed.), (CUP, 1924)
Sussex, Esther Meynell (Hale, 1947)
East Sussex, W. S. Mitchell (Shell Guides, 1978)
A Chalk Garden, Sir Frederick C. Stern (Faber, 1974)
The Archaeology of Gardens, Christopher Taylor (Shire Books, 1983)
The Seaboard and the Down, Revd John Wood Warter (Rivington, 1860)

Sussex County Magazine
Sussex Life
Sussex Notes and Queries

Sussex Archaeological Collections
Victoria County History of Sussex

West Sussex Record Office: Wiston Archives
                             Add. Mss. 10745–73

Charles Dalmon

Precise bibliographical information is difficult to obtain. It seems possible that the poet published some of his own work, of which at least four volumes remain: *Song Favours* (1895), *Singing as I Go* (1927), *Minutiae* and *A Poor Man's Riches*. No dates appear in the last two volumes.

Index

Ade, John, 35, 36
Ade, William, 35
Adur, River, 151, 165
Agricultural Board, 87
Agriculture, Ministry of, 88
Alciston, 121, 167
Alfred, King, 145
Alfriston, 35, 108, 128, 164
Althorp, 192
Amberley, 102; Wild Brooks, 102
Ancestors, 149
Angel Inn, 166
Anglo-Saxon Chronicle, 136, 144
Anne of Cleves' House, 184
Apuldram, 160
Ardingley, 164
Arnold Arboretum, 153
Arundel, 14, 16, 49, 103, 162–4, 176, 197, 200
Arundel Castle, 17, 103
Arundel; Cathedral of our Lady and St Philip Howard, 181
Ashcombe Toll House, 118

Baddings Tower, 133
Barnhorne Manor, 166
Barnhorn Manor, 166
Barnlands, 184
Bath Chronicle & Weekly Gazette, 190
Battle, 161
Battle Abbey, 121–2, 132, 133
Beachy Head, 25, 28, 38
Beecham, Sir Thomas, 84
Beeding, 165
Beggars Barn Shaw, 170
Belle Tout, 24–6, 73
Belloc, Hilaire, 171
Benedictines, 112, 132
Besborough, Lady, 194
Beynon, Revd, 108
Blackboys, 162
Black Death, 129
Blind houses, 66–7
Blith, Walter, 163

Bluebell Railway, 100–2
Blue Dick, 134
Blue Idol, 104–5, 110
Bodiam, 19, 74, 103, 123
Bodle Street Green, 169
Bognor Regis, 165
Bombay Bar, 176
Bopeep Farm, 167
Bosham, 14, 95, 141, 164, 203
Bostal Hill, 167
Bothiam, 203
Boulder Row, 37
Bow Hill, 28, 144–5
Boxgrove Abbey, 160, 200
Bracklesham Bay, 163
Bramber, 16, 29, 165
Bramber Castle, 16, 18, 112, 135
Bramber church, 134–6
de Braose, William, 18
Brede, 78, 98, 164
Brickwall, 113–15
Brighthelmstone, 162, 188
Brightling Down, 72
Brightling Needle, 72–3
Brightling Park, 71
Brighton, 51, 61, 118, 128, 140, 149, 162, 168, 175, 189 ff.
Brighton House, 189
British Petroleum, 48
Britten, Benjamin, 85
Bronze Age, 145
Brownbread Street, 162
Brown, Capability, 31, 151, 192
Browne, Sir Anthony, 132
Brunswick, Princess Caroline of, 195
Burpham, 134

Caburn, 29
Cackle Street, 161, 164
Calceto Farm, 197
Camber, 21
Canute, 96
Cap Mortella, 24
Carl Rosa Opera, 81, 82

Carlton House, 189, 191
Carthagena Farm, 163
Cassivellaunus, 143
Casson, Sir Hugh, 89
Castle Goring, 125–6, 128, 152
Cathedral of the Downs, 93, 95, 108, 110, 128, 164–5
Catt, William, 68–9
Cerne Abbas: Giant of, 34
Chailey, 88–9
Chailey Moat, 122–4
Chalk Pit Inn, 166
Chanctonbury, 29, 31–2, 172, 202
Chantry House, 116
Charleston Manor, 164
Charlton, 163
Chattri Memorial, 61
Chaucer, 110
Chichester, 14, 16–17, 28, 104, 129, 141, 144–5, 164, 179, 200
Chichester Castle, 21
Chichester Cathedral, 58, 77, 119, 120
Chichester Festival Theatre, 179
Chichester Market Cross, 75
Chichester Moon, 179
Chinoiserie, 193 ff.
Christie, George, 83–4
Christie, John, 79–84, 86
Church in a Wood, 164
Cinder Hill, 162
Cinque Ports, 98
Cissbury Ring, 29
Clapham, 57, 180
Clayton, 168
Clergy House, 108–10, 128
Clough, Roger, 30–1
Coadware, 72
Cobden, Richard, 166
Cochran, C. B., 184
Cocking, 166
Coconut Club, 189
Cokelers, 105–7
Coleridge, S. T., 193
Collier, Nathaniel, 54

Coolham, 104
Coopers Green, 161
Copper, Bob, 87
Corti, Walter, 88
Cowdray Castle, 132
Crawley, 40–1, 88, 139, 171
Creevey, Thomas, 188, 196
Crimean War, 59
Cromwell, Oliver, 129, 134–5
Cross-in-Hand, 163–4
Crusaders, 97, 163
Cuckmere Valley, 36, 128, 175
Cuckoo Day, 171
Cumberland, Duke of, 188–9
Curzon, Lord, 19
Cuthman, St, 28

Dallington, 62, 71
Dalmon, Charles, 170–5
Damon, William, 170
Danes, 17, 96, 144, 145
Deezes, 50
Denture, 162
Dependents, 105
Devil's Bumps, 28
Devil's Dyke, 28
Devil's Jumps, 28
Devonshiring, 163
Dew ponds, 42, 44–5
Dicul, 95–6
Didling, 170
Dissolution, 132
Ditchling, 28, 64, 184, 188
Dixter Manor, 113, 115
Dog Lane, 41
Domesday Book, 146
Downshire, Lady, 188
Dowsing, 134
Dunford House, 166

Easebourne, 164
Eastbourne, 24, 164, 166
East Dean, 52, 163
East Sussex, 17, 72, 77, 88, 163–4, 166
Ebourne, 166
Ecclesiastical Commissioners, 108
Edward the Confessor, King, 91
Edward I, King, 98
Edward VII, King, 175
Elizabeth I, Queen, 104, 112, 115–16, 162, 170, 201
Ellis, Dorothy, 112
Elsted, 91–2, 95, 167, 182
Eridge Rocks, 38, 39
Esso, 48
Etchingham, 139
Ewhurst, 75
Excise Officers, 73, 182

Faerie Queene, 80
Fairmile Bottom, 162
Farthings, 163
Ferrier, Kathleen, 85
Firle, 28
Firle House, 150–1
Fishbourne, 141, 160
Fiske, Billy, 200
Fitzalan, Richard, Earl of Arundel, 177
Fitzherbert, Mrs, 191 ff.
Five Lords' Burgh, 169
Folkestone, 24
Ford, 17
Forge Lane, 162
Foul Mile, 162
Foundry Meeting House, 75
Foxcombe Farm, 167
Friday Street, 164
Friston, 52
Fry, Revd Theodore, 78
Fuller, Mad Jack, 25–6, 52–3, 71–5
Funtington, 28, 164
Furnace Wood, 162

Gage family, 150–1
Gatwick, 164
Ginger's Green, 161
Gladstone, William, 58
Glasseye Farm, 161
Glyndebourne, 78–87
Goose Green, 167
Goring, Charles, 30–2, 202
Gotham, 167
Graffham, 57, 164
Great Wapses Farm, 160
Greene, Graham, 87
Green Gage, 150–1
Groombridge, 38
Grove House, 189
Gypsum, 61–3

Halifax, Baron, 26
Hammer ponds, 42
Hamper Green, 161

Harcourt, Hon. Mrs Vincent, 91–2
Harmer, Jonathan, 56, 202
Harold, King, 13, 132, 136
Harris, Jacob, 64
Harrison Rocks, 39
Hartfield, 60, 203
Harting, 64
Hartwell, 160
Hastings, 14, 16–17, 38, 49, 99, 127, 132, 136, 150, 164, 182–3, 199
Hawkhurst Mob, 74
Haye, Robert de la, 200
Hayes Hotel, 201
Heathfield, 46–8, 56, 65, 102, 118, 164, 171, 202
Hellingly Horselunges, 169
Henfield, 146–7
Hengrave Hall, 150–1
Henry I, King, 198
Henry III, 133
Henry VII, 51
Henry VIII, 20, 24, 41, 119, 120, 132, 162, 177, 185
Herbs, Roman, 142–3
Heritage Craft School, 88–9
Herstmonceux, 19, 40, 82
High and Over, 35
Highdown, 152–7, 167
Highnoons Farm, 169
High Rocks, 39
Hobbis, Eric, 36
Holland, Henry, 128, 192
Hollow Fields, 201
Holy Trinity, Bosham, 95–7
Horsham, 164
Horsham Slabs, 104, 110–12, 116, 141
Horsted Keynes, 101
Houghton Forest, 162
Hove, 140, 203
Howard, Catherine, 188
Huggett's Furnace, 162
Hundredsteddle, 170
Hyffold, 203

Ifield, 40, 164, 203
Iford, 164
Iron Brook, 162
Iron Duke, 139
Isfield, 164
Itford Hill, 164

Jack and Jill, 168
Jacob's Post, 64
Jellicoe, Basil, 124–5
Jessup, William, 167

INDEX

Jevington, 54
John, King, 21, 133
Julius Caesar, 13

Kaye-Smith, Sheila, 77
Kemp, Thomas, 191
Kemp Town, 191
Kew Gardens, 154
Kimmins, Dr, 89
Kimmins, Mrs, 89–90
Kingley Vale, 142–5
Kingston-near-Lewes, 52
Kipling, Rudyard, 171
Kissing gates, 179
Knights Templar, 112
Knockhundred Row, 169
Korchnoi, 184

Lancing College Chapel, 165
Land Gate, 133
Lavington, 57
Leonardslee, 44, 151, 165
Lewes, 16–17, 19, 37–8, 59, 67, 118, 122, 139, 163–4, 167, 175, 184, 187
Lewes Castle, 21
Liddell, Alice, 114
Lindfield, 184
Lish, Richard, 146–8
Litlington Village, 129
Little Bognor, 165
Little Doucegrove, 78
Little Heaven, 161
Little Knight's Oast, 163
Little London, 75, 104, 164
Little Slatters, 104–5
Little Twitten, 169
Lloyd, Nathaniel, 113
Longford stream, 123
Louise, Princess, Duchess of Argyll, 90
Loxwood, 105–7
Lullington church, 128–9
Lullington Court, 128–9, 203

Madamses Farm, 161
Maison Dieu, 176
Manning, Caroline, 57
Manning, Henry, 57–8
Mantrap, Lindfield, 184
Margaret, Beaufort, Countess of Richmond, 51, 52
Marine Pavilion, 128, 192 ff.
Marlborough, Duke of, 191
Martelli, Horatio, 24

Martello towers, 24
Martin, Edward, 44–5
Maundevild, 187
Meistersinger, 81
Michelham, 187, 198
Midhurst, 57, 132, 136, 166, 182
Mildred, Audrey, 82–6
Miles, Smoaker, 189
Minepit Wood, 162
Montgomery, Roger de, 14
Mortain, Robert, Count of, 18
Mortella, Cap, 24
Motte and bailey, 17–18
Moulsecoomb, 203
Mounsey, John, 81
Mozart, 188

Napoleon, 24, 88
National Trust, 19, 108–9
Natural gas, 47–8
Net shops, 50
Neville, Charles, 86–7
New Anzac on Sea, 86
New Gate, 99
Newhaven, 21, 26, 68
New York, 49, 50, 84
Ninfield, 64
Normans, 14, 119
Normanton, Helena, 51
Northiam, 66, 113–14, 163, 201–3
North Stoke, 134
Nyewood, 167

Oatlands Park, 89
Odo, Bishop of Bayeux, 13, 17
Offa, King of Mercia, 120
Offham, 163, 167
Offham Tramway, 167
Olafsson, Fridrik, 183–4
Old Savings Bank, 137
Old Treyford church, 92
Open Winkins, 162
Orleans, Philippe, Duc d', 193
Ouse, 26, 118

Pagden James, 35–6
Palace Chambers, 183
Parker, Ellis, 197–9, 203
Parkhouse, Revd F. J., 93, 182
Partridge Green, 161
Paymaster General's Office, 40

Peacehaven, 86–8, 97–8, 100
Peasmarsh, 114
Peelings, 163
Penn, William, 104
Pentchester, Stephen de, 98
Peppering Eye Farm, 161
Pestalozzi Village, 88–9
Pevensey, 13, 16–17, 21, 24, 38, 91, 166
Pevensey Castle, 17–18, 40, 95, 134, 167, 202–3
Piddinghoe, 118, 139
Pilgrim Fathers, 166
Pitt (the elder), 41
Pittsburg, 47–8
Plumpton, 45
Pondtail Copse, 69
Portsmouth, 26
Potter, Beatrix, 167
Potter's Green, 161
Pound Green, 161
Poverty Bottom, 162
Powell, Felix, 87
Preston Park, 140
Preventive Service, 183
Prince of Wales (future George IV), 168, 188 ff.
Puritans, 119
Pyecombe, 52, 139
Pynham Priory, 197 8

Quakers, 104–5
Queen Mother, Queen Elizabeth, 93

Racton Park, 26
Rapes of Sussex, 14, 18
Raptackle, 14
Rawnsley, Canon, 108
Rebecca, 125, 127–8, 132, 134
Reformation, 108, 119, 121
Richardson, John, 75
Riders Bolt, 169
Rivers, Lady Penelope, 150
Romans, 17, 95, 141, 145
Rose Hill, 71
Rottingdean, 86
Royal Greenwich Observatory, 19
Royal Institution, 71, 188
Royal Pavilion, 61, 128, 195 ff.
Royal Society, 45
Rushlake Green, 139
Russian Memorial, 59
Rye, 19, 21, 133, 139, 163

Saddlescombe, 66
St Anne's Well Gardens, 140
St Bartholomew's Church, 164
St Clement's Church, 24, 199
St John sub Castro, 59
St John the Baptist, 139
St Leonards', 78
St Mary's, 112
St Michael's Chapel, 183
St Michael's Church, 118
St Paul's Cathedral, 209
St Paul's Church, 91–3, 182
St Peter's Church, 92–3, 95, 164
St Philip Howard, 77, 181
St Richard, 110, 120, 125, 129
St Thérèse of Lisieux, 78
St Thomas' Church, 99
St Wilfrid, 77, 119
Sargent, Revd John, 57
Sassoon, Sir Albert, 175, 191
Saxon Cottage, 115
Saxons, 14, 17, 91, 95–6, 144–5
Seaford, 24
Sea Wolves, 144–5
Sedlescombe, 88–9, 115
Sefton, Dowager Lady, 196
Selmeston, 203
Selsey, 119
Seven Sisters, 28, 38
Shambledean, 45
Shaw, John, 104–5
Sheffield Park, 101
Shelley Monument, 57, 126–7
Shelley, Percy Bysshe, 128, 170
Shelley, Sir Bysshe, 125, 127–8, 132, 134
Sherbourne, Bishop Robert, 119
Sheridan, Richard Brinsley, 196
Sherwood Rough, 170
Shippons, 44
Shufflesheeps, 167
Sirgood, John, 105–6
Smirke, Robert, 71–2

Smith, Dr J. Douglas, 148
Smugglers' Cottage, 114
Snowdrop Inn, 37, 166
Society of Friends, 104–5
Somerley, 163
Sompting, 135–6
Southease, 118, 164
Southover, 184, 188
Sparks, 169
Speede, John, 98, 166, 203
Spence, Sir Basil, 51
Springwell, 41
Stane Street, 162
Stanmer Down, 45
Stanmer Park, 51
Stanstead Park, 26
Star Inn, Alfriston, 110–11
Star Inn, Heathfield, 102
Stern, Sir F. Claude, 152 ff.
Steyning, 29, 41, 115, 147, 203
Stony Beach, 50
Storey, Bishop, 75–7
Storrington, 41
Streat, 32
Subwealden Exploration, 47
Sugar Loaf, 72
Sussex Archaeological Society, 108, 113
Sussex Trust for Nature Conservation, 148
Sussex University, 51–2
Sussex Weekly Advertiser, 37
Swanbourne Lake, 161
Sweatings Lane, 161
Sweet Willow Shaw, 169

Tangmere, 200
Tapsell Gates, 52
Tarring Neville, 162
Tennyson, Alfred Lord, 171
Teorra, 162
Terrible Down, 162
Thomas, Edward, 170–2
Thorney Island, 160, 166
Three Bridges, 40
Three Cups Corner, 163–4
Tide Mills, 68–70
Tortington Priory, 197, 203
Treyford, 28, 92–3, 182, 203
Trotton, 167

Tudor, Queen Mary, 150
Turkey Island, 167
Turner, J. M. W., 71

Uckfield, 164
Udiam, 203
Uffington White Horse, 35
Upper Room, 78

Victoria, Queen, 32, 35, 197, 201
Village ponds, 42

Walberton, 53–4, 164
Walderton, 164
Warbleton, 164
Warminghurst Park, 30
Warninglid, 160, 165
Warr, Earl de la, 200
Weltje, Louis, 189 ff.
Wesley, John, 75
Westbourne, 166
West Dean, 163
Westdean, 163–4
Westham church, 134
West Sussex, 163–4, 166
White, Gilbert, 166
Whitehall, 26
White Rock, 182
White's Green, 161
Wight, Isle of, 197
Wilberforce, Samuel, 58
Wildham Wood, 169
William the Conqueror, 13–18, 38, 56, 91, 126, 132, 136, 150, 202
William IV, 197
Wilmington, Long Man of, 32, 34–5
Wilmington Priory, 122
Winchelsea, 19, 97–8, 150
Windfallwood Common, 160
Wish Tower, 24
Wiston, 29–31, 202
Wood, Mary, 147
W͘oods Mill, 145–7
woolton, Lord, 54
Worthing, 126, 157

Yeats, W. B., 116
Ypres Tower, 133